Table of Contents

Note: Much of this book consists of workbook pages for students to fill out for practice. The answers for these workbook pages can be accessed online at the link listed at the end of this book.

Mathematics

Chapter 1 - Place Value and Number Sense

Lesson 1

Finding Patterns

Draw the shape that comes next in the pattern.

1. ◯ ◦ ▢ ▫ △ △ _____

2. ▫ ▫ ▢ ◦ ◦ _____

3. ▢ △ ◯ ▢ △ ◯ ▢ △ _____

4. △ △ △ ◯ ◦ ◦ ▢ ▫ _____

5. ⬠ ◯ ▢ △ ⬠ ◯ ▢ △ _____

6. △ ▽ ▢ ▢ △ _____

7. ⬠ ◦ ◦ ⬠ △ △ △ ◯ ◯ _____

8. ⬠ ▢ △ ◦ ▫ △ ⬠ _____

Lesson 2

Even and Odd Numbers

 **Even numbers** are any number that can be divided exactly by 2.
Odd numbers are any number that can not be divided exactly by 2.

Are these numbers even or odd? Answer each question.

1. 4 _even_

2. 5 _____

3. 6 _____

4. 8 _____

5. 15 _____

6. 26 _____

7. 33 _____

8. 45 _____

9. 8 _____

10. 9 _____

11. 17 _____

12. 16 _____

13. 75 _____

14. 50 _____

15. 10 _____

16. 2 _____

17. 61 _____

18. 77 _____

19. 40 _____

20. 14 _____

21. 31 _____

22. 99 _____

23. 80 _____

24. 100 _____

Lesson 3

Rounding to the 100th

 Round the following numbers to the nearest hundred.

1. 285 ___300___
2. 863 _____
3. 262 _____
4. 83 _____
5. 211 _____
6. 819 _____
7. 828 _____
8. 144 _____
9. 751 _____
10. 373 _____
11. 305 _____
12. 267 _____
13. 611 _____
14. 996 _____

15. 150 _____
16. 326 _____
17. 356 _____
18. 704 _____
19. 740 _____
20. 508 _____
21. 164 _____
22. 771 _____
23. 266 _____
24. 238 _____
25. 753 _____
26. 194 _____
27. 789 _____
28. 333 _____

Lesson 4

Finding Patterns

Figure out what the numbers in each row have in common. Circle the number in each row that doesn't belong.

1. 10   20   30   (78)   50   60

2.   5   10   34   20   25   30

3.   2   4   15   8   10   12

4.   8   2   24   32   40   48

5.   3   5   7   8   9   11

6.   50   60   9   80   90   100

7.   55   65   75   85   95   3

8.   5   8   10   12   14   16

9.   3   5   7   9   11   89

Lesson 5

Place Value by 10's

All two digit whole numbers have a tens and a ones place.

Count the groups, then write the numbers.

1. = ___24___

2. = _____

3. = _____

4. = _____

5. = _____

6. = _____

Lesson 6

Place Value by 100's

All three digit whole numbers have a hundreds, tens and a ones place.

Hundreds	Tens	Ones
1	2	4

= 124

Count the groups, then write the numbers.

1. = __129__

2. = _____

3. = _____

4. = _____

5. = _____

Lesson 7

Least to Greatest

 Write these numbers from least to greatest.

1. 4,982   4,818   14,818   <u>4,818, 4,982, 14,818</u>

2. 1,900   880   1,251   _____

3. 1,541   1,210   1,780   _____

4. 129   74   50   _____

5. 3,500   815   1,520   _____

6. 5,800   3,400   9,570   _____

7. 100   1,000   10   _____

8. 4,500   5   330   _____

9. 250   275   300   _____

10. 54   25   16   _____

Lesson 8

Comparing Numbers

Compare the numbers. Write >,<, or = for each question.

1. 561 [>] 350

2. 1,234 [ ] 999

3. 3,500 [ ] 3,589

4. 85 [ ] 100

5. 5,329 [ ] 5,579

6. 1,050 [ ] 1,050

7. 28 [ ] 28

8. 674 [ ] 700

9. 2,300 [ ] 1,949

10. 2,012 [ ] 2,430

11. 4,259 [ ] 1,742

12. 330 [ ] 6,821

13. 4,120 [ ] 559

14. 165 [ ] 165

15. 50 [ ] 32

16. 832 [ ] 540

17. 1,100 [ ] 1,200

18. 2,180 [ ] 2,180

19. 6,432 [ ] 6,438

20. 2,451 [ ] 2,680

Chapter 2 - Addition

Lesson 1

2-Digit Addition - Regrouping

To add multiple digit numbers together, start in the ones place and then use basic addition rules. When the number equals ten or more the first digit carries over to the next spot. This is called **regrouping**.

	Hundreds	Tens	Ones
Step 1: Add the digits in the ones column.		8	5
	+ 1	7	
			[2]

	Hundreds	Tens	Ones
Step 2: Carry the 1 over to the top of the tens column.		1	
		8	5
x	1	7	
	①	2	

	Hundreds	Tens	Ones
Step 3: Add all the digits in the tens column together.		1	
	+ 8	5	
x	1	7	
	[1] [0]	2	

Solve the two-digit addition problems below.

1. 65
  + 14
   79

2. 35
  + 54

3. 11
  + 51

4. 42
  + 35

5. 89
  + 10

6. 25
  + 81

7. 47
  + 31

8. 12
  + 26

9. 25
  + 44

10. 51
  + 27

11. 19
  + 10

12. 13
  + 34

Lesson 2

Adding 3-Digit Numbers

Solve the three-digit addition problems below .

1. 910
   + 896
   ‾‾‾‾‾

2. 238
   + 654
   ‾‾‾‾‾

3. 336
   + 994
   ‾‾‾‾‾

4. 650
   + 273
   ‾‾‾‾‾

5. 852
   + 470
   ‾‾‾‾‾

6. 182
   + 649
   ‾‾‾‾‾

7. 238
   + 151
   ‾‾‾‾‾

8. 290
   + 764
   ‾‾‾‾‾

9. 905
   + 675
   ‾‾‾‾‾

10. 70
    + 134
    ‾‾‾‾‾

11. 436
    + 528
    ‾‾‾‾‾

12. 533
    + 343
    ‾‾‾‾‾

13. 866
    + 498
    ‾‾‾‾‾

14. 399
    + 249
    ‾‾‾‾‾

15. 615
    + 99
    ‾‾‾‾‾

16. 608
    + 422
    ‾‾‾‾‾

17. 206
    + 840
    ‾‾‾‾‾

18. 134
    + 428
    ‾‾‾‾‾

19. 704
    + 271
    ‾‾‾‾‾

Lesson 3

Fill in the Blanks

Fill in the blanks to complete each problem.

1. $\begin{array}{r} \underline{1}\ 2\ 4 \\ +\ 1\ 9\ \underline{1} \\ \hline 3\ 1\ 5 \end{array}$

2. $\begin{array}{r} 2\ \underline{}\ 9 \\ +\ \underline{}\ 3\ 2 \\ \hline 8\ 7\ 1 \end{array}$

3. $\begin{array}{r} 3\ 4\ 8 \\ +\ \underline{}\ 3\ \underline{} \\ \hline 9\ 7\ 9 \end{array}$

4. $\begin{array}{r} 6\ \underline{}\ 3 \\ +\ 2\ \underline{}\ 2 \\ \hline 8\ 4\ 5 \end{array}$

5. $\begin{array}{r} \underline{}\ 3\ 7 \\ +\ 4\ \underline{}\ 7 \\ \hline 5\ 8\ 4 \end{array}$

6. $\begin{array}{r} 5\ 8\ \underline{} \\ +\ \underline{}\ 9\ 1 \\ \hline 9\ 7\ 4 \end{array}$

7. $\begin{array}{r} 3\ 7\ 5 \\ +\ 1\ \underline{}\ \underline{} \\ \hline 5\ 8\ 0 \end{array}$

8. $\begin{array}{r} \underline{}\ 1\ 5 \\ +\ 1\ 2\ \underline{} \\ \hline 2\ 3\ 7 \end{array}$

9. $\begin{array}{r} \underline{}\ 2\ 4 \\ +\ 1\ 2\ 3 \\ \hline 5\ 4\ 7 \end{array}$

10. $\begin{array}{r} 5\ \underline{}\ 4 \\ +\ \underline{}\ 6\ 1 \\ \hline 7\ 8\ 5 \end{array}$

11. $\begin{array}{r} \underline{}\ 3\ 4 \\ +\ 1\ 6\ \underline{} \\ \hline 3\ 9\ 6 \end{array}$

Lesson 4

Addition Squares 1

- Add the numbers going down
- Add the numbers going across
- Then add your answers together, either across or down, to fill in the the last square

3	4	7
2	3	5
5	7	(12)

1.

1	5	
5	2	

2.

2	8	
8	9	

3.

6	3	
3	6	

4.

2	15	
15	2	

5.

25	4	
4	10	

6.

1	8	
8	40	

Chapter 3 - Subtraction

Lesson 1

Subtracting 2-Digit Numbers

To subtract and borrow, start with the ones column. If the bottom number is of a greater value, you have to borrow from the next column.

Step 1:	Tens	Ones	Step 2:	Tens	Ones	Step 3:	Tens	Ones
If the bottom number is a greater value than the top number, you need to borrow.	8	4	Borrow 10 from the next column. Reducing the 8 to 7 and increasing 4 to 14. Now we are ready to subtract.	7 8̸	¹4	Finish by subtracting the numbers in the tens column.	7 8̸	¹4
	− 1	9		− 1	9		− 1	9
					5		6	5

Solve the two-digit subtraction problems below.

1. 23
− 10
13

2. 86
− 81

3. 24
− 19

4. 65
− 29

5. 58
− 21

6. 42
− 12

7. 38
− 16

8. 37
− 15

9. 61
− 34

10. 57
− 43

11. 85
− 26

12. 82
− 39

- 16 -

Lesson 2

Subtracting 3-Digit Numbers

Solve the three-digit subtraction problems below .

1. 858
  − 830

2. 912
  − 875

3. 502
  − 436

4. 388
  − 346

5. 662
  − 136

6. 775
  − 163

7. 959
  − 436

8. 991
  − 519

9. 791
  − 113

10. 540
   − 162

11. 343
   − 278

12. 746
   − 141

13. 470
   − 129

14. 612
   − 129

15. 403
   − 246

16. 850
   − 773

17. 984
   − 623

18. 799
   − 486

19. 236
   − 149

Lesson 3

Subtraction Sentences

Complete the problems below by filling in the blank with the correct number.

1. ____ − 50 = 35

2. 45 - ____ = 13

3. ____ − 16 = 120

4. 66 - ____ = 24

5. ____ − 14 = 67

6. 109 - ____ = 56

7. ____ − 59 = 24

8. ____ − 31 = 42

9. ____ − 9 = 103

10. ____ − 72 = 2

11. 24 - ____ = 4

12. 89 - ____ = 28

13. 74 - ____ = 37

14. ____ - 56 = 104

15. 101 - ____ = 61

16. 98 - ____ = 41

17. ____ − 65 = 27

18. ____ − 3 = 13

19. ____ − 146 = 210

20. ____ − 0 = 30

Lesson 4

Borrow Over Two Zeros

Solve the three-digit subtraction problems below.

1. $\begin{array}{r} 400 \\ -\ 206 \\ \hline \end{array}$

2. $\begin{array}{r} 900 \\ -\ 309 \\ \hline \end{array}$

3. $\begin{array}{r} 300 \\ -\ 178 \\ \hline \end{array}$

4. $\begin{array}{r} 900 \\ -\ 107 \\ \hline \end{array}$

5. $\begin{array}{r} 700 \\ -\ 323 \\ \hline \end{array}$

6. $\begin{array}{r} 981 \\ -\ 100 \\ \hline \end{array}$

7. $\begin{array}{r} 806 \\ -\ 219 \\ \hline \end{array}$

8. $\begin{array}{r} 700 \\ -\ 386 \\ \hline \end{array}$

9. $\begin{array}{r} 800 \\ -\ 567 \\ \hline \end{array}$

10. $\begin{array}{r} 400 \\ -\ 205 \\ \hline \end{array}$

11. $\begin{array}{r} 900 \\ -\ 281 \\ \hline \end{array}$

12. $\begin{array}{r} 300 \\ -\ 86 \\ \hline \end{array}$

13. $\begin{array}{r} 200 \\ -\ 145 \\ \hline \end{array}$

14. $\begin{array}{r} 800 \\ -\ 734 \\ \hline \end{array}$

15. $\begin{array}{r} 774 \\ -\ 396 \\ \hline \end{array}$

16. $\begin{array}{r} 100 \\ -\ 54 \\ \hline \end{array}$

17. $\begin{array}{r} 800 \\ -\ 327 \\ \hline \end{array}$

18. $\begin{array}{r} 700 \\ -\ 605 \\ \hline \end{array}$

19. $\begin{array}{r} 300 \\ -\ 234 \\ \hline \end{array}$

Chapter 4 - Division

Lesson 1

Dividing Objects 1

Divide the objects equally by the animals for each group.

Objects	Animals	Answer
10 Bananas		5
15 Nuts		
9 Cheeses		
14 Bones		
20 Carrots		

Lesson 2

Division Wording and Terms

Complete each sentence.

1. $9\overline{)18}$ with 2 above is read " _18_ divided by _9_ is equal to _2_ ."

2. $4\overline{)16}$ with 4 above is read " ___ divided by ___ is equal to ___ ."

3. $5\overline{)125}$ with 25 above is read " ___ divided by ___ is equal to ___ ."

4. $15 \div 3 = 5$ is read " ___ divided by ___ is equal to ___ ."

5. $100 \div 10 = 10$ is read " ___ divided by ___ is equal to ___ ."

6. $72 \div 9 = 8$ is read " ___ divided by ___ is equal to ___ ."

7. $4\overline{)12}$ with 3 above The divisor is ____, the dividend is ____, the quotient is ____ ."

8. $5\overline{)30}$ with 6 above The divisor is ____, the dividend is ____, the quotient is ____ ."

9. $6\overline{)42}$ with 7 above The divisor is ____, the dividend is ____, the quotient is ____ ."

10. $8\overline{)64}$ with 8 above The divisor is ____, the dividend is ____, the quotient is ____ ."

11. $2\overline{)10}$ with 5 above The divisor is ____, the dividend is ____, the quotient is ____ ."

12. $3\overline{)21}$ with 7 above The divisor is ____, the dividend is ____, the quotient is ____ ."

Lesson 3

Dividing by 10 and 100

Use division to answer the following questions.

1. $70 \div 10 = \underline{7}$

2. $700 \div 100 = \underline{\hphantom{00}}$

3. $4600 \div 100 = \underline{\hphantom{00}}$

4. $5200 \div 100 = \underline{\hphantom{00}}$

5. $280 \div 10 = \underline{\hphantom{00}}$

6. $370 \div 10 = \underline{\hphantom{00}}$

7. $2700 \div 100 = \underline{\hphantom{00}}$

8. $330 \div 10 = \underline{\hphantom{00}}$

9. $220 \div 10 = \underline{\hphantom{00}}$

10. $990 \div 10 = \underline{\hphantom{00}}$

11. $5900 \div 100 = \underline{\hphantom{00}}$

12. $820 \div 10 = \underline{\hphantom{00}}$

13. $800 \div 10 = \underline{\hphantom{00}}$

14. $900 \div 10 = \underline{\hphantom{00}}$

15. $3000 \div 100 = \underline{\hphantom{00}}$

16. $970 \div 10 = \underline{\hphantom{00}}$

17. $460 \div 10 = \underline{\hphantom{00}}$

18. $950 \div 10 = \underline{\hphantom{00}}$

19. $590 \div 10 = \underline{\hphantom{00}}$

20. $650 \div 10 = \underline{\hphantom{00}}$

Lesson 4

Writing Division

Write out each problem and then solve it.

1. John has 24 toy planes. He wants to divide them into equal groups. Show two ways he can write that.

$$24 \div 8 = 3 \qquad 24 \div 6 = 4$$

2. Mary has 15 strawberries. She wants to divide them into equal groups. Show two ways she can write that.

_____   _____

3. Jane has 10 colors. She wants to divide them into equal groups. Show two ways she can write that.

_____   _____

4. Eric has 50 cards. He wants to divide them into equal groups. Show two ways he can write that.

_____   _____

Lesson 5

Basic Division 1

Solve each problem.

1. $9 \overline{)54}$ with answer 6

2. $4 \overline{)20}$

3. $4 \overline{)24}$

4. $3 \overline{)12}$

5. $8 \overline{)32}$

6. $9 \overline{)81}$

7. $2 \overline{)16}$

8. $7 \overline{)63}$

9. $3 \overline{)24}$

10. $7 \overline{)56}$

Lesson 6

Divide by 2 Both Ways

 Use division to answer the following questions.

1. $40 \div 2 = \underline{20}$ 2. $8 \div 2 = \underline{}$

3. $50 \div 2 = \underline{}$ 4. $30 \div 2 = \underline{}$

5. $12 \div 2 = \underline{}$ 6. $20 \div 2 = \underline{}$

7. $10 \div 2 = \underline{}$ 8. $50 \div 2 = \underline{}$

9. $38 \div 2 = \underline{}$ 10. $24 \div 2 = \underline{}$

11. $2 \overline{)44}$ 12. $2 \overline{)60}$

13. $2 \overline{)20}$ 14. $2 \overline{)84}$

15. $2 \overline{)12}$ 16. $2 \overline{)36}$

Lesson 7

Divide by 5 Both Ways

 Use division to answer the following questions.

1. $40 \div 5 = \underline{8}$
2. $90 \div 5 = \underline{}$

3. $50 \div 5 = \underline{}$
4. $30 \div 5 = \underline{}$

5. $15 \div 5 = \underline{}$
6. $20 \div 5 = \underline{}$

7. $10 \div 5 = \underline{}$
8. $50 \div 5 = \underline{}$

9. $35 \div 5 = \underline{}$
10. $25 \div 5 = \underline{}$

11. $5\overline{)85}$
12. $5\overline{)30}$

13. $5\overline{)65}$
14. $5\overline{)90}$

15. $5\overline{)105}$
16. $5\overline{)200}$

Lesson 8

Division Fill in the Blanks 1

Complete the following division problems by filling in the correct missing numbers.

1. $\underline{14} \div 2 = 7$

2. $15 \div \underline{} = 3$

3. $\underline{} \div 7 = 1$

4. $\underline{} \div 5 = 2$

5. $49 \div \underline{} = 7$

6. $54 \div \underline{} = 6$

7. $\underline{} \div 6 = 3$

8. $20 \div \underline{} = 2$

9. $25 \div \underline{} = 5$

10. $16 \div \underline{} = 4$

11. $\underline{} \div 6 = 6$

12. $12 \div \underline{} = 2$

13. $90 \div \underline{} = 9$

14. $\underline{} \div 9 = 4$

15. $45 \div \underline{} = 9$

16. $56 \div \underline{} = 8$

17. $\underline{} \div 10 = 10$

18. $40 \div \underline{} = 4$

19. $\underline{} \div 4 = 10$

20. $\underline{} \div 5 = 3$

Chapter 5 - Fractions

Lesson 1

Identifying Fractions

Color $\frac{1}{2}$ of each shape.

1.   2.   3.

Color $\frac{1}{3}$ of each shape.

4.   5.   6.

Color $\frac{1}{4}$ of each shape.

7.   8.   9.

Lesson 2

Explaining Fractions

A fraction names a part of a whole. It can also be used to name a part of a group or set.

Fractions are made up of two parts: the **numerator** and the **denominator**.

⬤ ◯ $\longrightarrow$ $\dfrac{1}{4}$ ◄——— The numerator is the number of shaded objects.
◯ ◯ ◄——— The denominator is the total number of objects.

Write what fraction of each set is shaded in.

1. ◯ ◯
    ◯ ⬤   = $\boxed{\dfrac{1}{4}}$

2. ⬤ ◯ ◯
    ⬤ ◯ ◯   = ☐

3. ⬤ ⬤ ◯ ◯
    ◯ ◯ ◯ ◯   = ☐

4. ◯◯◯◯◯
    ◯◯◯◯◯
    ◯⬤⬤⬤⬤   = ☐

5. ◼◼◼◼◻
    ◼◼◼◼◻   = ☐

6. ◼◼◼◼◻◻
    ◼◼◼◼◻   = ☐

7. ◼◼◻◻
    ◼◼◻◻
    ◼◻◻◻   = ☐

8. ◼◼◻◻◻
    ◼◼◼◻◻
    ◼◼◼◼◻   = ☐

Lesson 3

Matching Fractions

Draw a line to match the fractions.

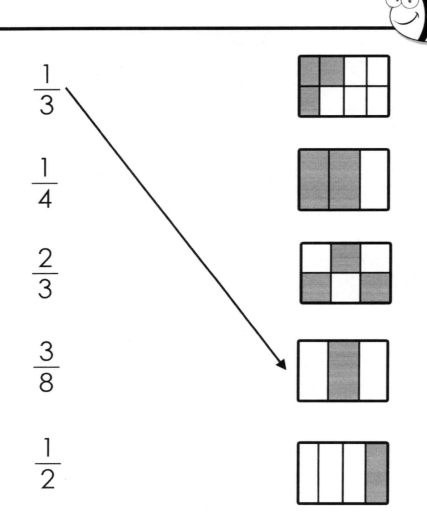

Lesson 4

Writing Fractions

Write the fraction shown in each shape.
Write the shaded amount as the top number.

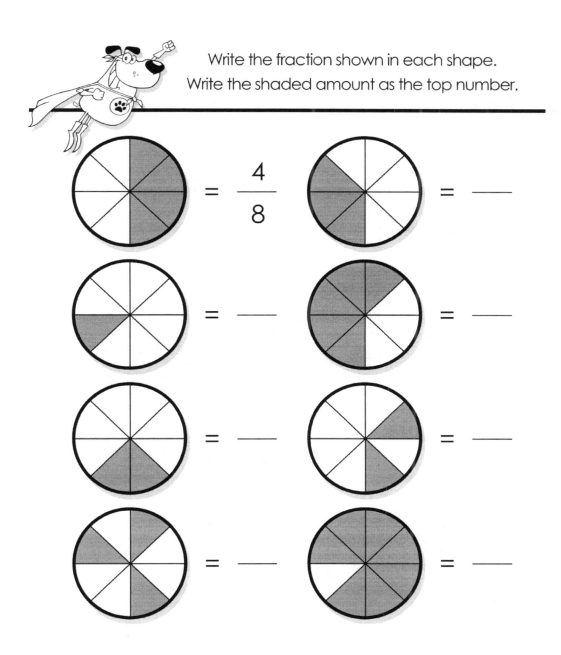

Lesson 5

Making Fractions

Color each shape to match the fraction.

$\dfrac{1}{4}$ =

$\dfrac{1}{2}$ =

$\dfrac{3}{8}$ =

$\dfrac{5}{8}$ =

$\dfrac{5}{16}$ =

$\dfrac{9}{16}$ =

$\dfrac{2}{16}$ =

$\dfrac{7}{16}$ =

Lesson 6

Whole Numbers and Fractions

The whole number **1** can be shown by many fractions.
When the numerator and denominator match, the fraction equals **1**.

$\dfrac{6}{6} = 1$	$\dfrac{8}{8} = 1$	$\dfrac{3}{3} = 1$

Any whole number can be shown as a fraction iby
using **1** for the denominator.

$2 = \dfrac{2}{1}$	$4 = \dfrac{4}{1}$	$9 = \dfrac{9}{1}$

Complete the fractions.

1. $1 = \dfrac{5}{5}$ **2.** $1 = \dfrac{}{8}$ **3.** $1 = \dfrac{3}{}$

4. $1 = \dfrac{}{14}$ **5.** $1 = \dfrac{6}{}$ **6.** $1 = \dfrac{}{10}$

Write the fraction that equals the whole number.

1. $5 = \dfrac{5}{1}$ **2.** $14 = \underline{}$ **3.** $9 = \underline{}$

4. $72 = \underline{}$ **5.** $3 = \underline{}$ **6.** $18 = \underline{}$

- 33 -

Lesson 7

Comparing Fractions

Just because two fractions are the same, that
does not mean they are the same amount.

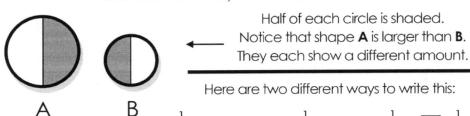

Half of each circle is shaded.
Notice that shape **A** is larger than **B**.
They each show a different amount.

A   B

Here are two different ways to write this:

$\frac{1}{2}$ of **A** is greater than $\frac{1}{2}$ of **B**   **OR** $\frac{1}{2}$ **A** $\boxed{>}$ $\frac{1}{2}$ **B**

Write out the fractions, then compare the fractions.

1.

$\frac{2}{6}$ $\boxed{<}$ $\frac{2}{4}$

2.

$\underline{\hphantom{00}}$ $\square$ $\underline{\hphantom{00}}$

2.

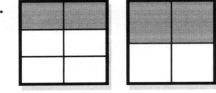

$\underline{\hphantom{00}}$ $\square$ $\underline{\hphantom{00}}$

2.

$\underline{\hphantom{00}}$ $\square$ $\underline{\hphantom{00}}$

Lesson 8

Choosing Fractions

Compare the fractions. Answer if each set is less than, greater than or equal.

$\dfrac{2}{8}$ < $\dfrac{4}{8}$ $\dfrac{1}{4}$ ☐ $\dfrac{2}{8}$

$\dfrac{2}{5}$ ☐ $\dfrac{3}{5}$ $\dfrac{5}{6}$ ☐ $\dfrac{2}{3}$

$\dfrac{1}{4}$ ☐ $\dfrac{1}{2}$ $\dfrac{2}{5}$ ☐ $\dfrac{1}{5}$

Chapter 6 - Multiplication

Lesson 1

Multiplication Rules

Multiplication is the way we find the sum of the same number a certain amount of times.

$4 \times 2 = 8$
$2 + 2 + 2 + 2 = 8$
□□ □□ □□ □□

$2 \times 5 = 10$
$5 + 5 = 10$
□□ □□
□□ □□
□ □

Break each group down by writing them out,
then adding them together.

1. $3 \times 2 = 6$

__ + __ + __ = __

2. $3 \times 4 = 12$

__ + __ + __ = __

3. $4 \times 4 = 16$

__ + __ + __ + __ = __

4. $4 \times 5 = 20$

__ + __ + __ + __ = __

5. $3 \times 8 = 24$

__ + __ + __ = __

6. $4 \times 10 = 40$

__ + __ + __ + __ = __

7. $2 \times 6 = 12$

__ + __ = __

8. $3 \times 6 = 18$

__ + __ + __ = __

Lesson 2

Multiplication by 1

The answer to a multiplication problem is called the **product**.

Switching the order doesn't matter. The product will always be the same.

1	1	1	1	1	1	1	1	1	1
x 0	x 1	x 2	x 3	x 4	x 5	x 6	x 7	x 8	x 9
0	1	2	3	4	5	6	7	8	9

0	1	2	3	4	5	6	7	8	9
x 1	x 1	x 1	x 1	x 1	x 1	x 1	x 1	x 1	x 1
0	1	2	3	4	5	6	7	8	9

Find the product.

1. 2	**2.** 4	**3.** 1	**4.** 9	**5.** 1	**6.** 6	**7.** 2
x 0	x 1	x 1	x 1	x 9	x 1	x 1
0						

8. 8	**9.** 1	**10.** 0	**11.** 3	**12.** 1	**13.** 1	**14.** 5
x 1	x 6	x 9	x 1	x 4	x 6	x 1

15. 3	**16.** 4	**17.** 1	**18.** 7	**19.** 1	**20.** 1	**21.** 0
x 1	x 0	x 2	x 1	x 8	x 7	x 1

Lesson 3

Multiplication by 2

The answer to a multiplication problem is called the **product**.

Switching the order doesn't matter. The product will always be the same.

| 2
x 0
0 | 2
x 1
2 | 2
x 2
4 | 2
x 3
6 | 2
x 4
8 | 2
x 5
10 | 2
x 6
12 | 2
x 7
14 | 2
x 8
16 | 2
x 9
18 |

| 0
x 2
0 | 1
x 2
2 | 2
x 2
4 | 3
x 2
6 | 4
x 2
8 | 5
x 2
10 | 6
x 2
12 | 7
x 2
14 | 8
x 2
16 | 9
x 2
18 |

Find the product.

| **1.** 9
x 2
18 | **2.** 2
x 4 | **3.** 8
x 2 | **4.** 1
x 7 | **5.** 2
x 9 | **6.** 2
x 5 | **7.** 7
x 1 |

| **8.** 2
x 2 | **9.** 3
x 2 | **10.** 2
x 3 | **11.** 9
x 2 | **12.** 8
x 1 | **13.** 2
x 7 | **14.** 5
x 2 |

| **15.** 0
x 2 | **16.** 2
x 6 | **17.** 8
x 2 | **18.** 5
x 0 | **19.** 4
x 1 | **20.** 2
x 1 | **21.** 8
x 1 |

Lesson 4

Multiplication by 3

The answer to a multiplication problem is called the **product**.

Switching the order doesn't matter. The product will always be the same.

| 3
x 0
0 | 3
x 1
3 | 3
x 2
6 | 3
x 3
9 | 3
x 4
12 | 3
x 5
15 | 3
x 6
18 | 3
x 7
21 | 3
x 8
24 | 3
x 9
27 |

| 0
x 3
0 | 1
x 3
3 | 2
x 3
6 | 3
x 3
9 | 4
x 3
12 | 5
x 3
15 | 6
x 3
18 | 7
x 3
21 | 8
x 3
24 | 9
x 3
27 |

Find the product.

1. 3
x 2
6

2. 9
x 0

3. 2
x 2

4. 2
x 7

5. 3
x 8

6. 4
x 3

7. 9
x 2

8. 3
x 8

9. 7
x 0

10. 2
x 8

11. 9
x 3

12. 7
x 3

13. 5
x 0

14. 3
x 3

15. 2
x 1

16. 7
x 1

17. 0
x 0

18. 5
x 3

19. 1
x 9

20. 3
x 5

21. 6
x 3

Lesson 5

Multiplication by 4

The answer to a multiplication problem is called the **product**.

Switching the order doesn't matter. The product will always be the same.

4	4	4	4	4	4	4	4	4	4
x 0	x 1	x 2	x 3	x 4	x 5	x 6	x 7	x 8	x 9
0	4	8	12	16	20	24	28	32	36

0	1	2	3	4	5	6	7	8	9
x 4	x 4	x 4	x 4	x 4	x 4	x 4	x 4	x 4	x 4
0	4	8	12	16	20	24	28	32	36

Find the product.

1. 3	**2.** 4	**3.** 4	**4.** 3	**5.** 1	**6.** 2	**7.** 0
x 1	x 0	x 5	x 4	x 4	x 8	x 3
3						

8. 7	**9.** 2	**10.** 1	**11.** 4	**12.** 4	**13.** 8	**14.** 4
x 4	x 4	x 2	x 9	x 5	x 4	x 1

15. 0	**16.** 6	**17.** 2	**18.** 3	**19.** 4	**20.** 6	**21.** 9
x 1	x 4	x 9	x 9	x 3	x 2	x 3

Lesson 6

Multiplication by 5

The answer to a multiplication problem is called the **product**.

Switching the order doesn't matter. The product will always be the same.

5	5	5	5	5	5	5	5	5	5
x 0	x 1	x 2	x 3	x 4	x 5	x 6	x 7	x 8	x 9
0	5	10	15	20	25	30	35	40	45

0	1	2	3	4	5	6	7	8	9
x 5	x 5	x 5	x 5	x 5	x 5	x 5	x 5	x 5	x 5
0	5	10	15	20	25	30	35	40	45

Find the product.

1. 4	**2.** 5	**3.** 7	**4.** 3	**5.** 0	**6.** 5	**7.** 6
x 3	x 2	x 5	x 6	x 5	x 1	x 3
12						

8. 8	**9.** 7	**10.** 2	**11.** 6	**12.** 5	**13.** 1	**14.** 9
x 5	x 0	x 8	x 5	x 5	x 4	x 5

15. 2	**16.** 8	**17.** 0	**18.** 5	**19.** 1	**20.** 5	**21.** 6
x 9	x 2	x 4	x 3	x 9	x 2	x 3

Lesson 7

Multiplication by 6

The answer to a multiplication problem is called the **product**.

Switching the order doesn't matter. The product will always be the same.

6 x 0 0	6 x 1 6	6 x 2 12	6 x 3 18	6 x 4 24	6 x 5 30	6 x 6 36	6 x 7 42	6 x 8 48	6 x 9 54

0 x 6 0	1 x 6 6	2 x 6 12	3 x 6 18	4 x 6 24	5 x 6 30	6 x 6 36	7 x 6 42	8 x 6 48	9 x 6 54

Find the product.

1. 0 x 6 0	**2.** 9 x 6	**3.** 5 x 3	**4.** 4 x 2	**5.** 6 x 2	**6.** 6 x 1	**7.** 2 x 7

8. 3 x 6	**9.** 6 x 6	**10.** 4 x 1	**11.** 6 x 5	**12.** 6 x 4	**13.** 6 x 0	**14.** 5 x 5

15. 3 x 9	**16.** 2 x 6	**17.** 5 x 6	**18.** 5 x 3	**19.** 6 x 8	**20.** 6 x 7	**21.** 6 x 0

Lesson 8

Multiplication by 7

The answer to a multiplication problem is called the **product**.

Switching the order doesn't matter. The product will always be the same.

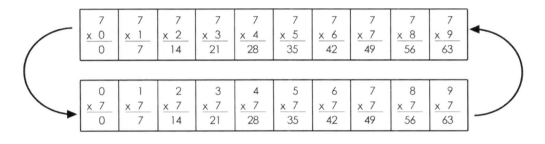

Find the product.

1. 4 x 3 12	**2.** 7 x 0	**3.** 4 x 5	**4.** 1 x 3	**5.** 7 x 6	**6.** 2 x 7	**7.** 3 x 3
8. 3 x 7	**9.** 7 x 9	**10.** 3 x 8	**11.** 7 x 4	**12.** 6 x 5	**13.** 1 x 4	**14.** 7 x 5
15. 7 x 2	**16.** 6 x 7	**17.** 7 x 1	**18.** 7 x 7	**19.** 7 x 8	**20.** 1 x 7	**21.** 6 x 7

Lesson 9

Multiplication by 8

The answer to a multiplication problem is called the **product**.

Switching the order doesn't matter. The product will always be the same.

| 8
x 0
0 | 8
x 1
8 | 8
x 2
16 | 8
x 3
24 | 8
x 4
32 | 8
x 5
40 | 8
x 6
48 | 8
x 7
56 | 8
x 8
64 | 8
x 9
72 |

| 0
x 8
0 | 1
x 8
8 | 2
x 8
16 | 3
x 8
24 | 4
x 8
32 | 5
x 8
40 | 6
x 8
48 | 7
x 8
56 | 8
x 8
64 | 9
x 8
72 |

Find the product.

| 1. 7
x 8
56 | 2. 4
x 4 | 3. 8
x 1 | 4. 2
x 6 | 5. 0
x 8 | 6. 7
x 5 | 7. 9
x 8 |

| 8. 3
x 5 | 9. 3
x 8 | 10. 6
x 0 | 11. 8
x 2 | 12. 5
x 5 | 13. 2
x 8 | 14. 8
x 7 |

| 15. 5
x 8 | 16. 8
x 9 | 17. 8
x 8 | 18. 4
x 8 | 19. 8
x 4 | 20. 5
x 2 | 21. 3
x 8 |

Lesson 10

Multiplication by 9

The answer to a multiplication problem is called the **product**.

Switching the order doesn't matter. The product will always be the same.

| 9
x 0
0 | 9
x 1
9 | 9
x 2
18 | 9
x 3
27 | 9
x 4
36 | 9
x 5
45 | 9
x 6
54 | 9
x 7
63 | 9
x 8
72 | 9
x 9
81 |

| 0
x 9
0 | 1
x 9
9 | 2
x 9
18 | 3
x 9
27 | 4
x 9
36 | 5
x 9
45 | 6
x 9
54 | 7
x 9
63 | 8
x 9
72 | 9
x 9
81 |

Find the product.

| 1. 9
x 1
9 | 2. 4
x 9 | 3. 8
x 7 | 4. 9
x 9 | 5. 3
x 7 | 6. 5
x 8 | 7. 9
x 1 |

| 8. 3
x 1 | 9. 6
x 4 | 10. 2
x 1 | 11. 6
x 9 | 12. 2
x 8 | 13. 7
x 5 | 14. 9
x 5 |

| 15. 9
x 4 | 16. 4
x 9 | 17. 0
x 9 | 18. 6
x 3 | 19. 3
x 7 | 20. 2
x 5 | 21. 3
x 9 |

Lesson 11

Multiplication Fill in the Blanks

In multiplication the numbers can be in any order.

Fill in the missing numbers.

1. $3 \times 2 = 6$
$2 \times \underline{3} = 6$

2. $4 \times 3 = 12$
$3 \times \underline{} = 12$

3. $5 \times 4 = 20$
$4 \times \underline{} = 20$

4. $1 \times 9 = 9$
$\underline{} \times 1 = 9$

5. $6 \times 3 = 18$
$3 \times \underline{} = 18$

6. $2 \times 5 = 10$
$5 \times \underline{} = 10$

7. $10 \times 5 = 50$
$5 \times \underline{} = 50$

8. $8 \times 4 = 32$
$4 \times \underline{} = 32$

9. $6 \times 6 = 36$
$\underline{} \times 6 = 36$

10. $7 \times 8 = 56$
$8 \times \underline{} = 56$

Lesson 12

Multiplication by 10

When multiplying a number by 10, multiply the number by one,
then bring down the zero.

$$\begin{array}{r} 10 \\ \times\ 8 \\ \hline 8 \end{array} \qquad \text{Then} \qquad \begin{array}{r} 10 \\ \times\ 8 \\ \hline 80 \end{array}$$

Solve the problems below.

1. $\begin{array}{r} 10 \\ \times\ 3 \\ \hline 30 \end{array}$ **2.** $\begin{array}{r} 10 \\ \times\ 2 \\ \hline \end{array}$ **3.** $\begin{array}{r} 10 \\ \times\ 5 \\ \hline \end{array}$ **4.** $\begin{array}{r} 10 \\ \times\ 6 \\ \hline \end{array}$ **5.** $\begin{array}{r} 10 \\ \times\ 1 \\ \hline \end{array}$

6. $\begin{array}{r} 10 \\ \times\ 5 \\ \hline \end{array}$ **7.** $\begin{array}{r} 10 \\ \times\ 4 \\ \hline \end{array}$ **8.** $\begin{array}{r} 10 \\ \times\ 8 \\ \hline \end{array}$ **9.** $\begin{array}{r} 10 \\ \times\ 7 \\ \hline \end{array}$ **10.** $\begin{array}{r} 10 \\ \times\ 0 \\ \hline \end{array}$

11. $\begin{array}{r} 10 \\ \times\ 9 \\ \hline \end{array}$ **12.** $\begin{array}{r} 10 \\ \times\ 2 \\ \hline \end{array}$ **13.** $\begin{array}{r} 10 \\ \times\ 4 \\ \hline \end{array}$ **14.** $\begin{array}{r} 10 \\ \times\ 3 \\ \hline \end{array}$ **15.** $\begin{array}{r} 10 \\ \times\ 9 \\ \hline \end{array}$

Lesson 13

Multiplication by 100

When multiplying a number by 100, multiply the number by one, then bring down the two zeros.

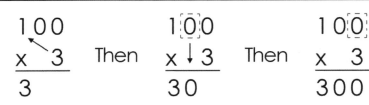

$$
\begin{array}{r} 100 \\ \times\ \ 3 \\ \hline 3 \end{array}
\quad \text{Then} \quad
\begin{array}{r} 100 \\ \times\ 3 \\ \hline 30 \end{array}
\quad \text{Then} \quad
\begin{array}{r} 100 \\ \times\ 3 \\ \hline 300 \end{array}
$$

Solve the problems below.

1. 100
x 4
___
400

2. 100
x 2

3. 100
x 5

4. 100
x 6

5. 100
x 1

6. 100
x 4

7. 100
x 8

8. 100
x 9

9. 100
x 0

10. 100
x 7

11. 100
x 3

12. 100
x 7

13. 100
x 4

14. 100
x 3

15. 100
x 9

Lesson 14

2-Digit Multiplication

To multiply a two-digit number by a one-digit number, you must first multiply the number in the one's place. Then you multiply the number in the ten's place.

Ten's	One's
3	2
x	3

→

Ten's	One's
3	2
x	3
	6

→

Ten's	One's
3	2
x	3
9	6

Solve the problems below.

1. 2 4
x 2
———
4 8

2. 7 3
x 3
———

3. 2 4
x 5
———

4. 6 4
x 2
———

5. 4 8
x 1
———

6. 6 3
x 1
———

7. 1 5
x 5
———

8. 5 4
x 2
———

9. 4 9
x 1
———

10. 3 8
x 2
———

Chapter 7 - Graphing

Lesson 1

Drawing a Graph 1

 Draw a line on the graph to answer each question.

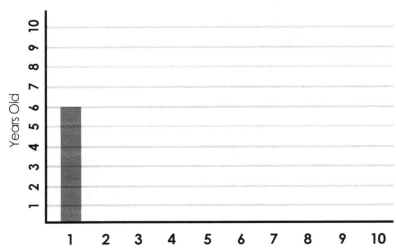

1. Tom is six years old.   **2.** Laney is seven years old.

3. Jane is two years old.   **4.** Stan is three years old.

5. Sally is one year old.   **6.** Mark is ten years old.

7. Mike is four years old.   **8.** Anne is eight years old.

9. Elle is five years old.   **10.** Donnie is nine years old.

Lesson 2

Reading a Graph

Use the graph to answer the questions.

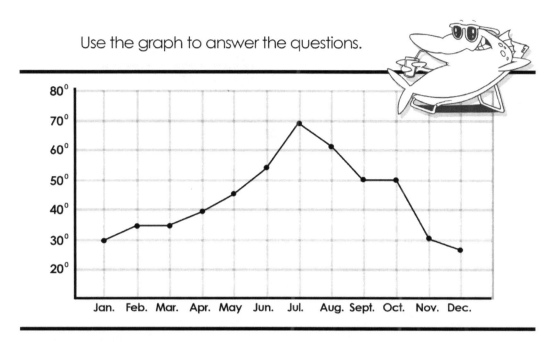

1. What was the coldest month? __December__

2. What was the hottest month? _____

3. What was the temperature in March? _____

4. About how many degrees was the difference between the coldest and hottest months? _____

5. What was the temperature in November? _____

6. Did it become hotter or colder from April to May? _____

7. Did the temperature change from September to October? _____

8. Which month was colder, January or December? _____

- 51 -

Lesson 3

Reading Pie Charts 1

Foods that families prefer.

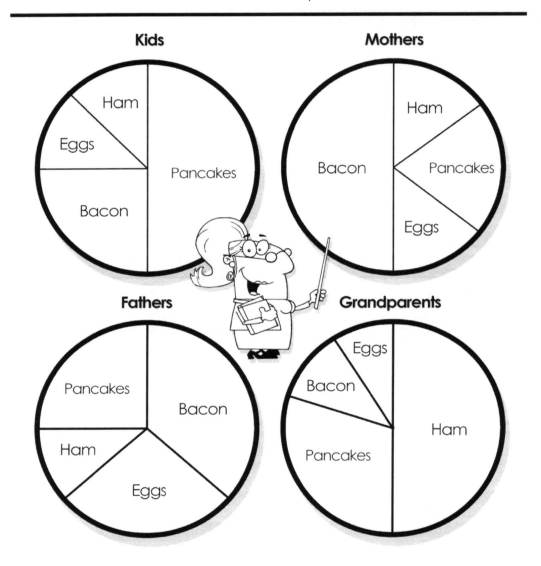

Reading Pie Charts 2

Use the pie charts on the last page
to answer the questions below.

1. Which breakfast food do kids like the most ? _____

2. Which breakfast food do grandparents like the most ? _____

3. Which breakfast food do mothers like the most? _____

4. Which breakfast food do fathers like the least? _____

5. What is the kids' second favorite food ? _____

6. What is the mothers' second favorite food ? _____

7. Which breakfast food do grandparents like least ? _____

Lesson 4

Drawing a Graph 2

Color in a square for each object you see in the picture below.

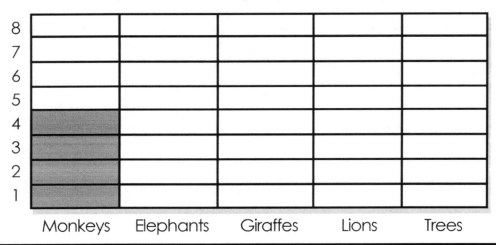

	Monkeys	Elephants	Giraffes	Lions	Trees
8					
7					
6					
5					
4	▓				
3	▓				
2	▓				
1	▓				

Lesson 4

Drawing a Graph - Matching Questions

Answer the questions using the graph you
just made on the last page.

1. How many giraffes are on the graph ?   3

2. How many elephants are on the graph ? _____

3. How many lions are on the graph ? _____

4. How many monkeys are on the graph ? _____

5. What is the sum of giraffes and lions ? _____

6. What is the difference of elephants and monkeys ?
_____

7. What is the product of lions times giraffes ? _____

Lesson 5

Word Problems and Graphs

Answer the questions by completing the chart.

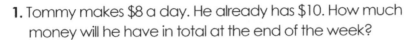

1. Tommy makes $8 a day. He already has $10. How much money will he have in total at the end of the week?

Tommy's Money	Monday	Tuesday	Wednesday	Thursday	Friday	Total
$10	$8	$8	$8	$8	$8	$50

2. Amy has walked 3 miles so far. If she walks 2 miles each day how many miles in total will she have walked at the end of the week?

Amy's Miles	Monday	Tuesday	Wednesday	Thursday	Friday	Total
3	2	2	2	2	2	_____

3. Jimmy has 12 pieces of candy. He buys 4 pieces each day. How much candy will he have in total at the end of the week?

Jimmy's Candy	Monday	Tuesday	Wednesday	Thursday	Friday	Total
12	4	4	4	4	4	_____

4. Cindy bakes cupcakes. She has 37 so far. She can bake 12 a day. How many will she have in total at the end of the week?

Cindys Cupcakes	Monday	Tuesday	Wednesday	Thursday	Friday	Total
37	12	12	12	12	12	_____

Lesson 6

Drawing Points on a Graph

Locate the points on the grid and draw the shapes for each question.

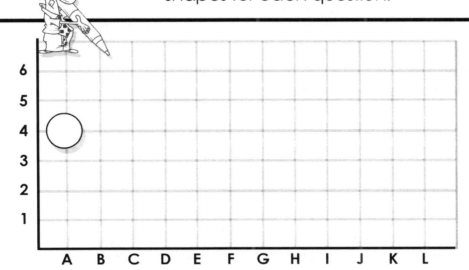

1. A, 4 - ◯

2. C, 1 - ⬡

3. K, 6 - △

4. H, 3 - ♡

5. F, 6 - ☆

6. L, 1 - ▱

Chapter 8 - Geometry & Measurements

Shapes

Lesson 1

Shape Counting 1

How many smaller shapes can you find in each larger shape? Write your answer.

2 ____   ____

____   ____

____   ____

____   ____

Lesson 2

Comparing Shapes by Sides

Write inside each shape how many sides it has.
Then answer each question.

1. (5) has how many more sides than [4] ? 1

2. (8) has how many more sides than (triangle) ? ____

3. How many total sides do you get when you add (trapezoid) with a (hexagon) ? ____

4. (8) has how many more sides than (7) ? ____

5. How many total sides do you get when you add (octagon) with a (triangle) ? ____

Lesson 3

Area

Area is the amount of space inside inside a shape.

Find the area of each shape.

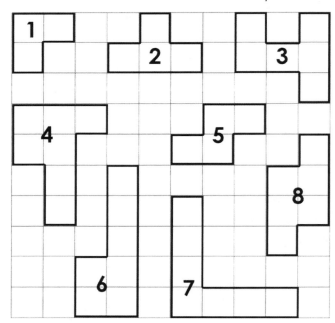

1. __3__ Units   5. _____ Units

2. _____ Units   6. _____ Units

3. _____ Units   7. _____ Units

4. _____ Units   8. _____ Units

Lesson 4

Perimeter

Perimeter is the distance around an object.
Find the perimeter of each object by adding all the sides.
Write out the equation.

1.

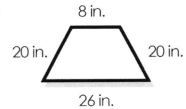

6 in.

4 in.　　　　4 in.

6 in.

$4 + 6 + 4 + 6 = 20$ in.

2.

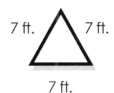

7 ft.　　7 ft.

7 ft.

_____

3.

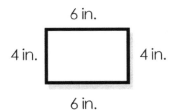

8 in.

20 in.　　　　20 in.

26 in.

_____

4.

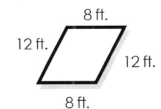

8 ft.

12 ft.　　　　12 ft.

8 ft.

_____

5.

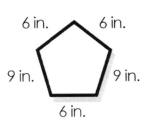

6 in.　　6 in.

9 in.　　　　9 in.

6 in.

_____

6.

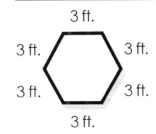

3 ft.

3 ft.　　　　3 ft.

3 ft.　　　　3 ft.

3 ft.

_____

Lesson 5

Lines and Line Segments

A point is an exact location in space.   •

A line is an endless straight path.   ⟷

A line segment is a straight path between two points.   A •——————• B

Name if each figure is a point, line or line segment.

1.   Line segment

2.   •   _____

3.   _____

4.   _____

Use the drawing below to answer the questions.

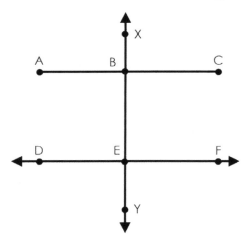

1. Name a line   _____

2. Is AC a line or a line segments?
_____

3. Name a point   _____

4. Is DF a line or a line segments?
_____

5. At what point does line DF cross line XY? _____

Lesson 6

Angles

Angles are where two lines meet.

We measure angles in degrees. To write an angle, we use the degree symbol "⁰". **_Example: 90⁰_**

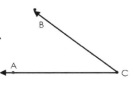

The measurement of an angle determines its name.

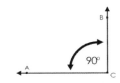	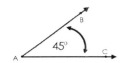	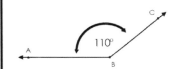
An angle that is exactly 90⁰ is a **right angle**.	An angle that is less than 90⁰ is an **acute angle**.	An angle that is more than 90⁰ is an **obtuse angle**.

Name the types of angles.

1.  _____

2.  _____

3.  _____

4.  _____

Lesson 7

Weight Measurements

Two ways weight can be measured is in ounces and pounds.

We use **ounces** to measure the weight of lighter objects.
We use **pounds** to measure the weight of heavier objects

 = **9** ounces   = **15** pounds

Circle whether each object should be
measured using ounces or pounds.

1.

Ounces
Pounds

2.

Ounces
Pounds

3.

Ounces
Pounds

4.

Ounces
Pounds

5.

Ounces
Pounds

6.

Ounces
Pounds

Lesson 8

Distance Measurements

1 foot = **12** inches
1 yard = **3** feet or **36** inches
1 mile = **1,760** yards

Answer the questions and tell whether each question should
use measurement units of a foot, yard or mile

1. The length of a soccer field should be measured in __yards__.

2. Tommys' height should be measured in _____.

3. The distance from home to school is measured in _____.

4. The basketball goal is 10 _____ tall.

5. Steven can jump 3 _____.

6. The distance between the earth and moon is measured
   in _____.

7. The tree in the yard is 22 _____ tall

8. A football field is measured in _____.

9. Roads are measured in _____.

10. A 12 inch ruler is a _____ long.

Lesson 9

Liquid Measurements

1 Cup | 1 Pint | 1 Quart | 1 Gallon

| 2 Cups = 1 Pint | 2 Pints = 1 Quart | 4 Quarts = 1 Gallon |

Circle how much liquid each container can hold.

1.  (1 Cup) / 1 Quart

2.  1 Cup / 1 Gallon

3.  1 Cup / 1 Pint

4.  1 Quart / 1 Cup

5.  1 Pint / 1 Quart

6.  1 Gallon / 1 Cup

Practice Test #1

Practice Questions

1. Jillian writes the number: 860,002. Which of the following represents this number, in words?

Ⓐ Eight hundred sixty thousand, twenty

Ⓑ Eight hundred sixty thousand, two

Ⓒ Eight hundred sixty two thousand

Ⓓ Eight hundred six thousand, two

2. Arlan compares his annual electricity expenses over a five-year time span. His annual expenses are shown in the table below.

Year	Expense
2007	$1,224
2008	$1,319
2009	$1,046
2010	$1,529
2011	$1,342

Which of the following shows the years listed, in order, from lowest electricity expense to highest electricity expense?

Ⓐ 2009, 2008, 2007, 2010, 2011

Ⓑ 2007, 2009, 2011, 2010, 2008

Ⓒ 2009, 2007, 2011, 2008, 2010

Ⓓ 2009, 2007, 2008, 2011, 2010

3. Wyatt's coach passed out balls to the entire team. One-third of the balls Wyatt received were basketballs. Which of the following could represent the balls he received?

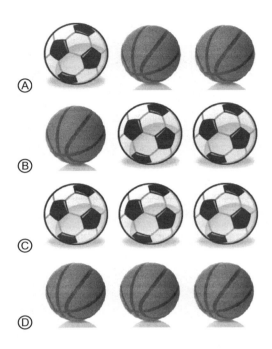

Ⓐ

Ⓑ

Ⓒ

Ⓓ

4. What number sentence is illustrated by the diagram below?

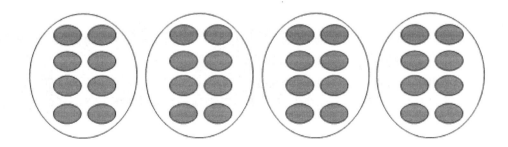

Ⓐ $32 \times 4 = 128$

Ⓑ $32 - 4 = 28$

Ⓒ $32 \div 4 = 8$

Ⓓ $32 + 4 = 36$

5. Which three statements below can be represented by the expression 6 × 5?

Circle the correct answers.

    I.   A student has 6 pieces of gum and 5 pieces of candy.

    II.   A teacher gives 6 students 5 books each.

    III.   There are 5 students playing on the playground and 6 more join them.

    IV.   There are 6 cars and each one is carrying 5 people.

    V.   There are 5 rows of chairs in the auditorium with 6 chairs per row.

6. Kristen must buy three items that are priced at $4.58, $6.22, and $8.94. What is the best estimate for the total cost of all three items?

   Ⓐ $18

   Ⓑ $16

   Ⓒ $20

   Ⓓ $22

7. Which of the following represents $\frac{2}{3}$?

Ⓐ

Ⓑ

Ⓒ

Ⓓ

- 69 -

8. On Monday, David finished gluing 96 tiles in 8 hours. On Tuesday, he finished gluing 72 tiles in 8 hours. Which of the following is a possible first step in determining how many more tiles he glued per hour on Monday?

Ⓐ Add the number of tiles glued each day

Ⓑ Subtract the number of hours it took to glue the tiles from the number of tiles glued

Ⓒ Multiply the number of hours spent gluing tiles on Monday by the number of hours spent gluing tiles on Tuesday

Ⓓ Divide the number of tiles glued each day by the number of hours it took to glue them

9. At the birthday party, each guest received 12 game tokens and each game takes 2 tokens. If there were 8 guests at the party, how many tokens were given out?

_____

Part B: How many games could be played?

_____

10. James drew the following connected squares and labeled them as Figure 1, Figure 2, and so on.

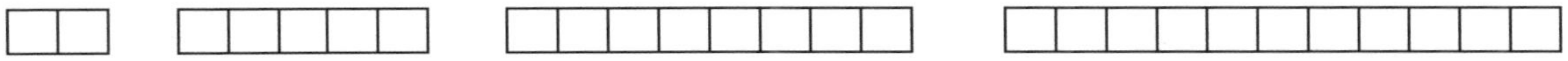

Figure 1 Figure 2   Figure 3   Figure 4

If he continues this pattern, how many squares will he use for Figure 9?
- Ⓐ 21
- Ⓑ 23
- Ⓒ 26
- Ⓓ 29

11. A teacher donates to a local charity. Each year, she donates three times the amount donated the previous year. If the teacher donated $2 the first year, how much did she donate during the fifth year?
- Ⓐ $158
- Ⓑ $164
- Ⓒ $162
- Ⓓ $144

12. Fill in the blanks below to complete the equation.

___ × 3 = 12

16 − ___ = 10

8 + ___ = 17

13. A class collects spiders. Spiders have 8 legs each. Which table shows the number of legs found on the spiders brought to class?

Ⓐ

Number of Spiders	Number of Legs
2	10
3	11
6	14
8	16
11	19

Ⓑ

Number of Spiders	Number of Legs
4	28
5	35
9	63
12	84
14	98

Ⓒ

Number of Spiders	Number of Legs
3	12
4	13
8	17
10	19
12	21

Ⓓ

Number of Spiders	Number of Legs
3	24
5	40
6	48
9	72
12	96

14. The total number of candy pieces found in different numbers of candy jars is shown in the table below.

Number of Candy Jars	Number of Candy Pieces
2	28
4	56
5	70
9	126

How many candy pieces are there in 13 candy jars?

Ⓐ 154

Ⓑ 168

Ⓒ 182

Ⓓ 196

15. Penny drinks 8 glasses of water each day. The number of glasses of water she drinks over a 12-day time span can be determined, using the number sentence: $8 \times 12 = ?$
Which number sentence would not show the number of glasses of water she drinks?

Ⓐ $? \div 8 = 12$

Ⓑ $12 \times 8 = ?$

Ⓒ $? \div 12 = 8$

Ⓓ $12 - 8 = ?$

16. Belinda draws a rectangle with a length of 6 cm and a width of 2 cm. She draws a second rectangle with a length of 9 cm and a width of 5 cm, and she draws a third rectangle with a length of 7 cm and a width of 3 cm. Draw a line to match the rectangle with its correct area.

45 Sq. Ft.	Rectangle 1
18 Sq. Ft.	
21 Sq. Ft.	Rectangle 2
12 Sq. Ft.	
35 Sq. Ft.	Rectangle 3

17. Which of the following figures is NOT congruent to the others shown?

Ⓐ

Ⓑ

Ⓒ

Ⓓ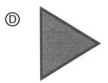

18. Which number is greater than the number shown by Point M on the number line?

Ⓐ 12 ¼

Ⓑ 12 ½

Ⓒ 12

Ⓓ 12 ¾

19. Which of the following shapes has 6 faces? Select all that apply.

I. Square pyramid
II. Triangular prism
III. Cube
IV. Triangular pyramid
V. Rectangular prism

20. Which of the following is congruent to the shape shown below?

Ⓐ

Ⓑ

Ⓒ

Ⓓ

- 76 -

21. Part A: What number does Point P represent?

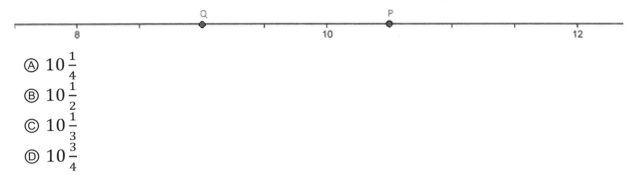

Ⓐ $10\frac{1}{4}$

Ⓑ $10\frac{1}{2}$

Ⓒ $10\frac{1}{3}$

Ⓓ $10\frac{3}{4}$

Part B: How much bigger is the number represented by point P than the number represented by Point Q?

Ⓐ $1\frac{1}{2}$

Ⓑ $\frac{2}{3}$

Ⓒ 1

Ⓓ $\frac{3}{4}$

22. What is the perimeter of the figure shown below?

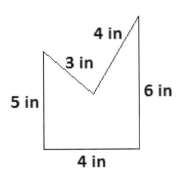

Ⓐ 20 in

Ⓑ 22 in

Ⓒ 24 in

Ⓓ 21 in

23. What is the perimeter of the trapezoid shown below?

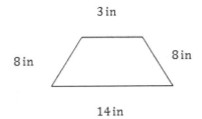

Ⓐ 28 in

Ⓑ 31 in

Ⓒ 34 in

Ⓓ 33 in

24. The rectangle below has a length that is three times its width. What is the length of this rectangle?

6 in.

Ⓐ 10 in

Ⓑ 14 in

Ⓒ 18 in

Ⓓ 20 in

25. How many square units are found in the trapezoid below?

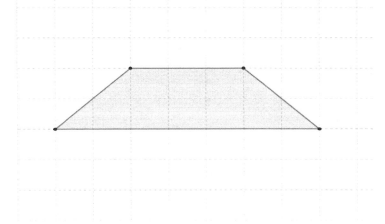

Ⓐ 8 square units

Ⓑ 12 square units

Ⓒ 10 square units

Ⓓ 9 square units

26. Which of the figures below is shaded to represent $\frac{5}{8}$?

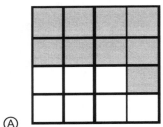
Ⓐ

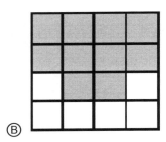
Ⓑ

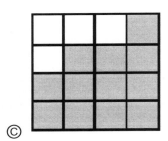
Ⓒ

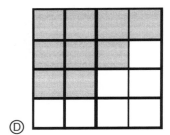
Ⓓ

27. To get ready for school in the morning Ashley does the following:

- Takes 6 minutes to get dressed
- Takes 7 minutes to fix her hair
- Takes 12 minutes to eat breakfast
- Brushes her teeth for 2 minutes

What is the total time it takes her to get ready for school in the morning?

_____

28. The bar graph below shows the number of zoos found in four states.

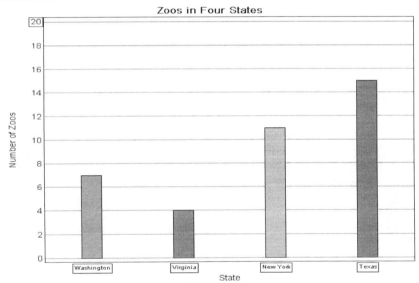

Which state has the most zoos?

Ⓐ Washington

Ⓑ Virginia

Ⓒ New York

Ⓓ Texas

29. A fish bowl contains 2 striped, 4 orange, and 2 blue fish. Eli randomly scoops a fish from the bowl. Which of the following statements is true?

Ⓐ He is less likely to scoop an orange than a striped fish

Ⓑ He is more likely to scoop a striped than a blue fish

Ⓒ He is more likely to scoop a blue than an orange fish

Ⓓ He is equally likely to scoop a striped and a blue fish

30. Which expression below has the same value as $23 + 48 + 32$?

Ⓐ $20 + 40 + 32 + 2 + 3 + 8$

Ⓑ $3 + 8 + 2 + 4 + 2 + 3$

Ⓒ $20 + 40 + 30 + 3 + 2 + 4 + 8$

Ⓓ $40 + 20 + 30 + 3 + 8 + 2$

31. Which of the following shapes has 5 fewer lines of symmetry than an octagon?

Ⓐ

Ⓑ

Ⓒ

Ⓓ

32. What is the perimeter of the triangle shown below?

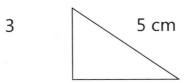

3   5 cm

4 cm

Ⓐ 6 cm

Ⓑ 12 cm

Ⓒ 9 cm

Ⓓ 8 cm

33. Which of the following is the best estimate for the distance from the center of the circle, marked C, to a point on the circle?

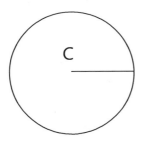

C

Ⓐ 2 cm

Ⓑ 12 cm

Ⓒ 5 cm

Ⓓ 8 cm

34. A crayon is shown below. Use the ruler from your mathematics chart to measure the length of the crayon. About how long is the crayon, from base to tip, to the nearest inch?

Ⓐ 2 in

Ⓑ 3 in

Ⓒ 4 in

Ⓓ 5 in

35. The number of lawns, finished by four different landscaping companies, in one week, is shown in the table below.

Landscaping Company	Number of Lawns
Landscaping Company A	12
Landscaping Company B	18
Landscaping Company C	6
Landscaping Company D	16

Which pictograph shows the number of lawns finished by each company?

Ⓐ

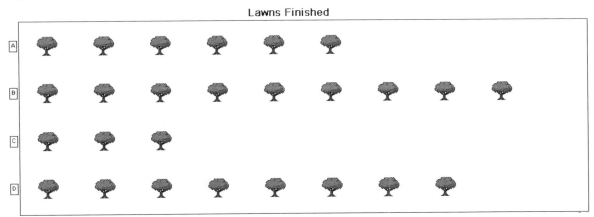

Each tree represents 2 lawns.

Ⓑ

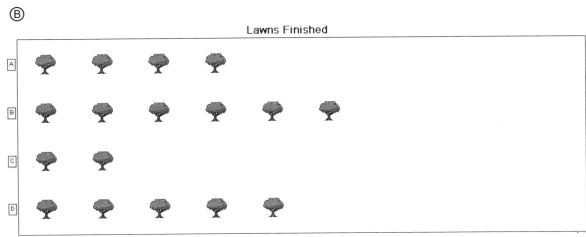

Each tree represents 4 lawns.

Ⓒ

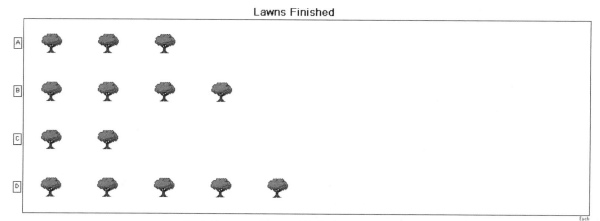

Each tree represents 2 lawns.

Ⓓ

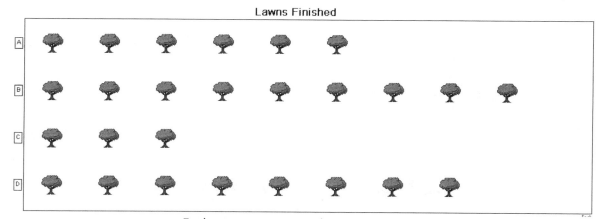

Each tree represents 3 lawns.

36. Which clock below would be read as a five o'clock?

Ⓐ **5:00**

Ⓑ **5:30**

Ⓒ **5:05**

Ⓓ **5:55**

37. Aubrey rolls a die. Which of the following statements is true?

Ⓐ She is more likely to roll a 3 than a 6

Ⓑ She is equally likely to roll a 3 or a 6

Ⓒ She is less likely to roll a 3 than a 6

Ⓓ She is certain to roll a 3 or a 6

Answers and Explanations

1. B: The number, 860,002 has an 8 in the hundred-thousands place, a 6 in the ten-thousands place, a 0 in the thousands place, a 0 in the hundreds place, a 0 in the tens place, and a 2 in the ones place. The 860 written in front of the comma represents, "Eight hundred sixty thousand." The 2 in the ones place represents, "Two." Therefore, the number is read, "Eight hundred sixty thousand, two."

2. D: The annual expenses for Years 2009, 2007, 2008, 2011, and 2010 are $1,046, $1,224, $1,319, $1,342, and $1,529, respectively. These amounts are listed in order from lowest to highest. Since all of the numbers have a 1 in the thousands place, the numerals in the hundreds place must be compared. For the amounts of $1,319 and $1,342, the numerals in the tens place must be compared. No other choice shows the years listed in increasing order of expense.

3. B: If 1/3 of the balls Wyatt received were basketballs that means the remaining balls he received must have been soccer balls. Since the fraction used is 1/3, look at it as if he received 3 balls. One ball was a basketball and the remaining balls had to be soccer balls. This is now a simple subtraction problem. 3 – 1 = 2 soccer balls.

4. C: The diagram shows 32 counters divided into 4 groups, with 8 counters in each group. Therefore, the total number of counters, 32, is divided by 4, giving a quotient of 8, which is written as: $32 \div 4 = 8$.

5. I, IV,V: All of these statements can represent 6×5 because they all have 6 groups that contain 5 of something. The other two choices represent $6 + 5$.

6. C: The item priced at $4.58 can be rounded to $5. The item priced at $6.22 can be rounded to $6. The item priced at $8.94 can be rounded to $9. The sum of 5, 6 and 9 is 20. Thus, the best estimate is $20.

7. B: Choice B shows 4 shaded sections out of 6 total sections. The fraction, $\frac{4}{6}$, is the same as the fraction, $\frac{2}{3}$. Two shaded sections represent one-third of the total. Thus, four shaded sections represent two-thirds of the total. Each of the pictures has 6 total sections, so the other choices can be written as fractions with a 6 in the denominator. Choice A shows $\frac{3}{6}$, which equals $\frac{1}{2}$. Choice C shows . Choice D shows $\frac{2}{6}$, which equals $\frac{1}{3}$. So, only Choice B shows the correct picture.

8. D: A possible first step would be to divide the number of tiles glued each day by the number of hours it took to glue the tiles. The two quotients would then represent approximately how many tiles glued per hour, and could then be compared.

9. Part A: 96: There are 8 guests at the party that each receives 12 tokens. $8 \times 12 = 96$

Part B: 48: If each game requires 2 tokens to play then the number of games that can be played can be found by dividing the total number of tokens by 2. $96 \div 2 = 48$

10. C: Each figure has 3 more squares than the previous figure, so adding 3 to the number of squares in the previous figure yields the number of squares in the next figure. Thus, he will use 14 squares for Figure 5, 17 squares for Figure 6, 20 squares for Figure7, 23 squares for Figure 8, and 26 squares for Figure 9.

11. C: In order to find the amount donated the following year, you multiply the amount donated the previous year by 3. Thus, the amount donated the second year was $6 ($2 × 3). The amount donated the third year was $18 ($6 × 3). The amount donated the fourth year was $54 ($18 × 3). The amount donated the fifth year was $162 ($54 × 3).

12. The first answer is 4, because $4 \times 3 = 12$, and this can be found by rearranging the equation to $12 \div 3 =$ ___. The second answer is 6, because

$16 - 6 = 10$, and this can be found by rearranging the equation to $16 - 10 = \_\_$. The last answer is 9, because $8 + 9 = 17$, and this can be found by rearranging the equation to $17 - 8 = \_\_$.

13. D: Each spider has 8 legs. In order to find the number of legs present with 3 spiders, you multiply 3 by 8, which is 24. Thus, 3 spiders have 24 legs in all. Choice D is the only table that shows each number of spiders, multiplied by 8, to yield the correct product representing the total number of legs.

14. C: Each candy jar has 14 pieces of candy. This can be determined by dividing the number of pieces of candy by the number of candy jars: $28 \div 2 = 14, 56 \div 4 = 14, 70 \div 5 = 14, 126 \div 9 = 14$. Since the data in the table shows that there are 14 pieces of candy in each jar, multiplying $13 \times 14 = 182$ finds the total number of pieces of candy that are in 13 candy jars.

15. D: If she drinks 8 glasses of water each day, the number of glasses of water she drinks in 12 days can be determined by multiplying 8 by 12. This product is 96; thus she drinks 96 glasses of water in a 12-day time span. The relationship between the number of glasses of water she drinks per day and the total number of glasses of water she drinks in 12 days can be represented by an appropriate multiplication or division number sentence within the following fact family: $8 \times 12 = 96, 96 \div 8 = 12, 12 \times 8 = 96, 96 \div 12 = 8$. Subtracting 8 from 12 will not reveal the number of glasses she drinks in a 12-day time span. The number sentence: $12 - 8 = ?$, is not in this fact family.

16. The answer should look like:

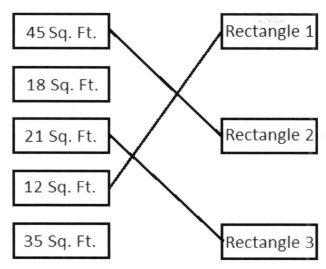

17. D: Choices A, B, and C are all the same right triangle just flipped around. Answer choice D is a different triangle and therefore not congruent.

18. D: 12 ¼ is represented by the first tick mark to the right of the 12. 12 ½ is the second tick mark and 12 ¾ is the third tick mark, or the tick mark before the 13. Only 12 ¾ appears to the right of point M on the number line, making it greater.

19. III, V : A face of a shape is each individual surface. Only a cube and a rectangular prism have 6 faces.

20. D: The trapezoid shown for Choice D is congruent to the given shape, provided. Basically, the shapes must be the same size to be congruent, but can be flipped or rotated in any way.

21. Part A: B: Each increment represents one-half. This can be determined by counting that there are 3 marks, or 4 spaces, that lie between the difference of two wholes, as in between 10 and 12. Thus, one increment past 10, where Point P is located, represents $10\frac{1}{2}$.

Part B: A: Point Q is at 9, so the difference between Point P and Point Q is $1\frac{1}{2}$.

22. B: The perimeter is the distance around the figure. So, if you add up all of the numbers you get 22 in.

23. D: The perimeter of the trapezoid is the distance around all of the sides, and is equal to the sum of 3 in, 8 in, 8 in, and 14 in. Thus, the perimeter is 33 in.

24. C: The width of the rectangle is given as 6 in., and the length can be found by multiplying that times 3. $6 \times 3 = 18$

25. C: The trapezoid has 8 square units, plus 4 one-half square units, which equals 2 more square units. The sum of 8 square units and 2 square units is 10 square units.

26. B: There are 16 small squares in total. This means that for $\frac{5}{8}$ of them to be shaded there would need to be 10 of them shaded.

27. 27: To find out how long it takes Ashley to get ready just add up all of the minutes that she spends doing various activities. $6 + 7 + 12 + 2 = 27$

28. D: Texas has the most zoos because it has 15 zoos, while the other states each have 7 zoos, 4 zoos, and 11 zoos. Also, it can be seen from the graph that the bar representing Texas is much higher than the bars for the other states.

29. D: The more fish there is of a certain color the more likely it is that the color of fish is scooped. With more orange fish than striped fish in the bowl, he is more likely to scoop an orange fish than a striped one. There are equal amounts of striped and blue fish, so one is not more likely than the other. There are more orange fish than blue fish, so he is more likely to scoop an orange fish than a blue one.. Finally, the number of striped and blue fish is the same – so they are equally likely to be scooped compared to each other. Thus, Choice D is the only true statement.

30. D: This answer just breaks down the first equation. It adds all of the 10's places first, then adds all of the 1's places.

31. B: An octagon has 8 lines of symmetry, and 3 lines of symmetry is 5 fewer than 8 lines of symmetry. An equilateral triangle (Choice B) has 3 lines of symmetry, while a square (Choice A) has 4 lines of symmetry, a pentagon (Choice C) has 5 lines of symmetry, and an isosceles trapezoid (Choice D) has 1 line of symmetry. Thus, an equilateral triangle is the only shape shown that has 5 fewer lines of symmetry than an octagon.

32. B: The distance around the triangle, or the perimeter, is equal to the sum of 3 cm, 5 cm, and 4 cm. Thus, the perimeter is 12 cm.

33. A: The distance from the center of the circle, marked C, to a point on the circle, is also known as the radius, and it is approximately 2 cm. The distance can be estimated by marking off estimated units of length for a centimeter. Such markings approximate 2 centimeters.

34. B: The crayon measures almost exactly 3 inches.

35. A: Since each tree represents 2 lawns, the pictograph shows that the number of lawns finished by Company A is equal to 6 × 2, or 12 lawns, the number of lawns finished by Company B is equal to 9 × 2, or 18 lawns, the number of lawns finished by Company C is equal to 3 × 2, or 6 lawns, and the number of lawns finished by Company D is equal to 8 × 2, or 16 lawns. This is the only pictograph that represents the correct number of lawns.

36. A: Five o'clock shown on a digital clock would be shown as a 5 followed by two zeroes, indicating no minutes.

37. B: Since a die has one of each number, from 1 to 6, she is equally likely to roll any of the six numbers. The possibility of rolling one of these numbers is no more or less than the possibility of rolling another of these numbers. Thus, she is equally likely to roll a 3 or a 6.

Practice Test #2

Practice Questions

1. Which of the following is an expression for five subtracted from twenty-five equals twenty?

Ⓐ 25 - 20 = 5

Ⓑ 5 - 25 = 5

Ⓒ 25 - 5 = 20

Ⓓ 20 + 5 = 25

2. Bercu sells 128 hot dogs this month. She sold 117 hot dogs last month. How many hot dogs has she sold in these past two months?

Ⓐ 235

Ⓑ 241

Ⓒ 242

Ⓓ 245

3. Which of the following answers are the same as 6×8? Select all that apply.

   I. $2 \times 3 \times 8$

  II.   6 groups of 8 apples

 III. $4 \times 2 \times 8$

 IV.   8 people join another group of 6 people

  V.   6 people each have 8 t-shirts

4. Fill in the blanks to complete the equation.

$7 \times \underline{\quad} = 28$

$\underline{\quad} + 9 = 22$

$18 - \underline{\quad} = 5$

5. Farm A has 8 chickens and 3 horses. Farm B has 6 chickens and 5 horses. Which of the following is a possible first step in determining which farm contains more animal feet?

Ⓐ Multiply the number of chickens on each farm by 2, and multiply the number of horses on each farm by 4

Ⓑ Find the total number of animals found on both farms

Ⓒ Multiply the sum of the number of chickens and horses, found on both farms, by 6

Ⓓ Add 2 to the number of chickens found on each farm, and add 4 to the number of horses found on each farm

6. Which model shows a fraction that is more than 4 out of 7?

Ⓐ

Ⓑ

Ⓒ

Ⓓ

7. The number of miles Jacob has walked each year over the past five years is shown in the table below.

Year 1	691
Year 2	567
Year 3	144
Year 4	963
Year 5	221

Which sequence of years shows the number of miles he walked each year, listed in order from greatest to least?

Ⓐ Year 2, Year 4, Year 5, Year 1, Year 3

Ⓑ Year 4, Year 1, Year 2, Year 5, Year 3

Ⓒ Year 1, Year 4, Year 2, Year 5, Year 3

Ⓓ Year 3, Year 2, Year 5, Year 4, Year 1

8. A neighborhood contains 4 streets. Street 1 has 23 houses, Street 2 has 12 houses, and Street 3 has 34 houses. Estimate by rounding, how many houses are in this neighborhood?

Ⓐ 40

Ⓑ 50

Ⓒ 60

Ⓓ 70

9. Which of the following fractions are bigger than $\frac{5}{8}$? Select all that apply.

I. $\frac{5}{9}$

II. $\frac{5}{6}$

III. $\frac{3}{4}$

IV. $\frac{1}{2}$

V. $\frac{4}{10}$

10. A farmer plants rows of corn each growing season. The table below shows the total number of rows of corn the farmer has planted after several seasons.

Season	Number of Rows
Season 2	34
Season 4	68
Season 6	102
Season 7	119
Season 10	

How many rows of corn will the farmer have planted by the end of Season 10?

Ⓐ 153

Ⓑ 170

Ⓒ 136

Ⓓ 168

11. What is the area of the figure shown below?

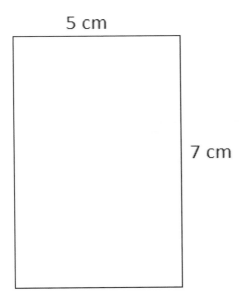

5 cm

7 cm

---

12. Anand has 45 stamps in his collection. He decides to give all of his stamps to 5 friends. He writes the number sentence below to find out how many stamps to give each friend, if each friend is to receive an equal amount.

$$45 \div 5 = ?$$

Which number sentence would NOT help him find the number of stamps to give each friend?

Ⓐ $? \times 5 = 45$

Ⓑ $45 - 5 = ?$

Ⓒ $45 \div ? = 5$

Ⓓ $5 \times ? = 45$

13. The table below shows the number of books students brought to share with the class.

Number of Students	Number of Books
2	8
5	20
6	24
8	32

How many books did 12 students bring?

    Ⓐ 44

    Ⓑ 36

    Ⓒ 40

    Ⓓ 48

14. Which figure has 6 vertices?

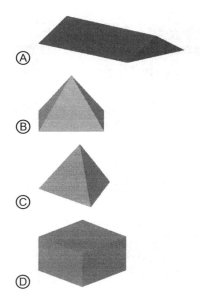

15. Plot a point on the number line below that represents $14\frac{1}{2}$.

```
├────┬────┬────┬────┬────┬────┬────┬────┬────┬────┬────┬────┤
    12            13            14            15
```

16. What statement is NOT true about the figure below?

Ⓐ It has 5 vertices

Ⓑ It has 6 edges

Ⓒ It is a pyramid

Ⓓ It has 5 faces

17. Kerrie has 152 stickers. She decides to give 34 of them away to friends. Then she goes to the store and buys 67 more stamps. How many stamps does she have now?

_____

18. Which of the following figures has fewer than 5 faces?

Ⓐ Triangular pyramid

Ⓑ Triangular prism

Ⓒ Cube

Ⓓ Rectangular pyramid

19. Which figure does not have a line of symmetry?

Ⓐ

Ⓑ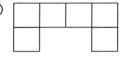

Ⓒ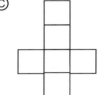

Ⓓ

20. Part A: The figure below is divided into what fraction?

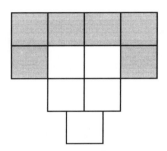

Ⓐ tenths

Ⓑ twelfths

Ⓒ elevenths

Ⓓ thirteenths

Part B: What fraction is shaded in?

Ⓐ $\frac{5}{10}$

Ⓑ $\frac{5}{11}$

Ⓒ $\frac{6}{11}$

Ⓓ $\frac{6}{12}$

21. What is the perimeter of the pentagon shown below?

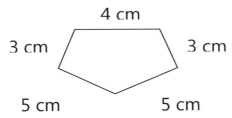

4 cm

3 cm   3 cm

5 cm   5 cm

Ⓐ 29 cm

Ⓑ 20 cm

Ⓒ 15 cm

Ⓓ 25 cm

22. A student compares the perimeter of a triangle, a square, a rectangle, and a hexagon. The triangle has side lengths of 3 cm, 5 cm, and 6 cm. The square has a side length of 4 cm. The rectangle has a length of 3 cm and a width of 4 cm. The hexagon has six equal side lengths of 2 cm. Which of these shapes has the largest perimeter?

Ⓐ Triangle

Ⓑ Square

Ⓒ Rectangle

Ⓓ Hexagon

23. Part A: Each day at school Billy spends 30 minutes reading. How many minutes will he read in 6 days?

_____

Part B: If each book takes an hour to read, how many books can he read in those 6 days?

_____

24. Steve bought 7 watermelons at the store. The total weight of the watermelons was 28 pounds. If each water melon weighed the same amount, how much did one watermelon weigh?

Ⓐ 7 pounds

Ⓑ 4 pounds

Ⓒ 5 pounds

Ⓓ 3 pounds

25. Part A: A rectangle has a width of 7cm and a length of 9cm. What is its perimeter?

_____

Part B: What is the area of the rectangle?

_____

26. John walks from his house to the grocery store in 9 minutes. When he leaves the grocery store it takes him 12 minutes to walk to the dry cleaners. When he leaves there he decides to walk through the park on his way home, and it takes him 23 minutes to get home. How many minutes did John walk from the time he left his house until he returned home?

Ⓐ 32 minutes

Ⓑ 42 minutes

Ⓒ 44 minutes

Ⓓ 34 minutes

27. A bag contains 3 red cards, 7 blue cards, 9 green cards, and 6 yellow cards. Jesse randomly draws a card from the bag. Which of the following statements is true?

Ⓐ He is less likely to draw a green card than a yellow card

Ⓑ He is more likely to draw a yellow card than a red card

Ⓒ He is more likely to draw a yellow card than a blue card

Ⓓ He is equally likely to draw a red, blue, green, or yellow card

28. A student spins a spinner, with sections, labeled 1 – 8. Which of the following best represents the likelihood of the spinner landing on a 9?

Ⓐ Likely

Ⓑ Not likely

Ⓒ Certain

Ⓓ Impossible

29. The bar graph below shows the number of Math teachers, from four different states, attending a math event.

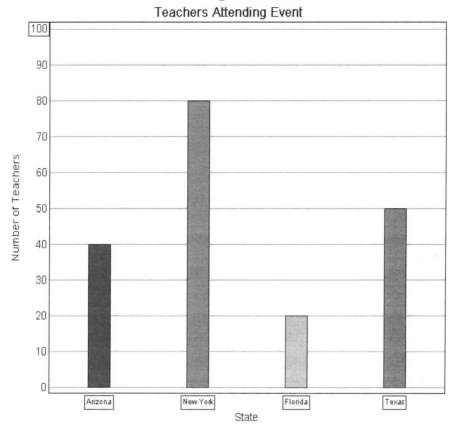

Which state has the fewest number of teachers attending the math event?

Ⓐ Arizona

Ⓑ New York

Ⓒ Florida

Ⓓ Texas

30. The bar graph below shows the number of votes for choosing a class mascot.

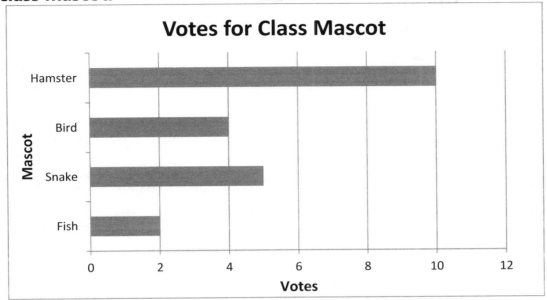

How many more votes did the hamster receive than the fish?

---

31. Hannah builds the towers shown below, using square blocks.

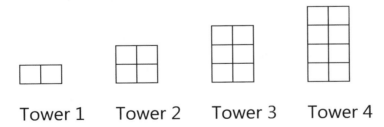

Tower 1   Tower 2   Tower 3   Tower 4

If she continues this pattern, how many square blocks will she use in the eighth tower?

- Ⓐ 12
- Ⓑ 16
- Ⓒ 18
- Ⓓ 14

32. Which of the following are true? Select all that apply.

    I. $4 \times 11 = 40$

    II. $32 - 9 = 23$

    III. $\dfrac{4}{5} = \dfrac{8}{10}$

    IV. $7 \times 9 = 61$

    V. $\dfrac{3}{8} = \dfrac{6}{4}$

33. A pencil is shown below. Use the ruler from your mathematics chart to measure the length of the pencil. About how long is the pencil, from base to tip, to the nearest inch?

Ⓐ 2 in

Ⓑ 3 in

Ⓒ 4 in

Ⓓ 5 in

34. Amanda arrives at a birthday party at the time shown on the clock below.

What time did she arrive at the party?

Ⓐ 10:10

Ⓑ 2:10

Ⓒ 9:10

Ⓓ 2:50

35. The outside temperature, on a spring day, in Flagstaff, Arizona, is shown on the thermometer below.

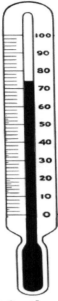

What is the temperature, in degrees Fahrenheit?

Ⓐ 77° F

Ⓑ 76° F

Ⓒ 79° F

Ⓓ 74° F

36. A candy bowl contains 3 chocolates, 7 peppermints, and 4 lollipops. Adeline randomly draws a piece of candy from the bowl. Which of the following statements is true?

Ⓐ She is less likely to draw lollipop than a chocolate

Ⓑ She is more likely to draw a chocolate than a peppermint

Ⓒ She is more likely to draw a peppermint than a lollipop

Ⓓ She is equally likely to draw a chocolate, peppermint, or a lollipop

37. Jordan wants to show the number of wheels found on several cars. Which table should he use?

Ⓐ

Number of Cars	Number of Wheels
3	12
4	16
7	28
11	44
12	48

Ⓑ

Number of Cars	Number of Wheels
2	6
5	15
8	24
9	27
12	36

Ⓒ

Number of Cars	Number of Wheels
3	15
5	25
6	30
8	40
11	55

Ⓓ

Number of Cars	Number of Wheels
4	8
6	12
9	18
12	24
14	28

Answers and Explanations

1. C: The term subtracted from means to "take away" and place a minus sign in the equation. Since 5 is being subtracted from 25, write the number 25 first followed by a minus sign and then the number 5. The problem states that this subtraction equals 5, so simply attach this to the end.

2. D: In order to find out the total number of hot dogs she sold in the two months, the amount sold in each month should be added. The sum of 128 and 117 is 245. Thus, she sold 245 hot dogs during the two months.

3. I, II, V: $2 \times 3 = 6$, so that makes that I. the same. II and V are both 6 groups of 8, which is the same as 6×8.

4. The first one is 4. To find this rearrange the equation to $28 \div 7 = 4$. The second one is 13. To find this rearrange the equation to $22 - 9 = 13$. The last one is 13. To find this rearrange the equation to $18 - 5 = 13$.

5. A: Since a chicken has 2 feet and a horse has 4 feet, you may multiply the number of chickens found on each farm by 2, and then multiply the number of horses found on each farm by 4. After finding the total number of chicken feet and horse feet on each farm, you can then add the two amounts to find the total number of animal feet on each farm. You can then compare the two values to determine the one that is larger.

6. B: Each model shows a whole, split into 7 sections. This makes the denominator equal to 7 for the fraction representing the shaded section for each. Since the fractions all have the same number on the bottom, the number of shaded sections can be compared. For a fraction to be more than $\frac{4}{7}$, more than 4 parts must be shaded. The model shown for Choice B shows the fraction $\frac{6}{7}$, because 6 out of 7 sections are shaded, showing a fraction that is more than 4 out of 7. The other choices all show either 4 parts or less than 4 parts shaded.

7. B: The sequence of the number of miles walked in order from greatest to least is: 963 (Year 4), 691 (Year 1), 567 (Year 2), 221 (Year 5), 144 (Year 3). The number of miles walked can also be compared by examining only the digits in the hundreds place since they are all different. 9 is greater than 6 which is greater than 5 and so on. The only choice that shows the years for the number of miles walked in descending order is B.

8. D: 23 + 12 + 34 = 69. Since the 9 in the ones digit is greater than or equal to five, the number is rounded up to 70.

9. II and III: To figure out which one is bigger first you need to find a common denominator. The least common denominator of 6 and 8 is 24. So, convert $\frac{5}{8}$ to $\frac{15}{24}$, and $\frac{5}{6}$ to $\frac{20}{24}$, and you see that $\frac{5}{6}$ is bigger. The $\frac{3}{4}$ can just be converted to $\frac{6}{8}$, and you can see that it is bigger than $\frac{5}{8}$.

10. B: The farmer plants 17 rows of corn each season. This can be found using all of the information given in the table. The farmer had planted 34 rows of corn by the end of Season 2 and 68 rows of corn by the end of Season 4, indicating an increase of 34 rows of corn between the two seasons. So, by dividing 34 by 2, the numbers of rows planted in one season is found. Also, the farmer had planted 102 rows of corn by the end of Season 6 and 119 rows of corn by the end of Season 7, indicating an increase of 17 rows of corn planted in one season. If 17 rows of corn are added to the number given at the end of Season 2, the result is 51 rows of corn planted by the end of Season 3. If another 17 rows of corn are added to this amount, the farmer would have planted 68 ears of corn by the end of Season 4, which he did. Thus, he did plant 17 rows of corn each year. He had planted 136 rows of corn by the end of Season 8, 153 rows of corn by the end of Season 9, and 170 rows of corn by the end of Season 10.

11. 35 cm: To find the area of a rectangle just multiply the length times the width.

12. B: A number sentence that subtracts the number of friends from the total number of stamps will not provide the number of stamps needed to give each friend. Instead, an appropriate multiplication or division number sentence within the following fact family is needed: $9 \times 5 = 45$, $5 \times 9 = 45, 45 \div 9 = 5$, or $45 \div 5 = 9$.

13. D: The number of books brought by 2 students is 8, while the number of books brought by 5 students and 6 students increased by 4. Thus, the number of books brought by each student was 4. This fact can be checked by starting with 1 student and 4 books brought, and continuing the pattern to make sure it corresponds with the numbers in the table. For example, 8 students brought 32, which does in fact agree with the each student bringing 4 books. So, the number of books each student brought, 4, is multiplied by the number of students to find the total number of books that were brought. Thus, 12 students brought 12×4 books, or 48 books.

14. A: A vertex is a point where two or more edges meet. So, a triangular prism (Choice A) has 6 vertices, while a square pyramid (Choice B) has 5 vertices, a triangular pyramid (Choice C) has 4 vertices, and a cube (Choice D) has 8 vertices. Thus, the triangular prism is the only figure with 6 vertices.

15. Each tick mark on the number line represents a change of $\frac{1}{4}$. The number line below shows the correct placement of the point.

16. B: The figure shown is a square pyramid. It indeed has 5 vertices and 5 faces. It has 8 edges, not 6 edges, so Choice B is the only statement that is not true.

17. 185: She starts with 152 stickers and then gives 34 away. So, 152-34=118. Then she buys 67 more, which gives her 118+67=185.

18. A: A triangular pyramid (Choice A) has 4 faces, while a triangular prism (Choice B) and a rectangular pyramid (Choice D) both have 5 faces. A cube

(Choice C) has 6 faces. Thus, the only figure with less than 5 faces is the triangular pyramid.

19. D: Figures A, B, and C can all be folded in a manner that the squares lay directly on top of each other. This cannot be done with Figure D; therefore, Figure D does not have a line of symmetry.

20. Part A: C: If you count all of the boxes you see that the figure is divided into 11 pieces.

Part B: C: Now count the boxes that are shaded in and you get 6, so $\frac{6}{11}$ are shaded.

21. B: The perimeter is the sum of the lengths of all five sides, or $5 + 5 + 3 + 3 + 4$, which equals 20. Therefore, the perimeter of the pentagon is 20 cm.

22. B: To find the perimeter of each shape, add up the lengths of all of the sides. The square has four sides of equal length, so it has a perimeter of 16 centimeters, which is larger than the perimeters of the other three shapes. The triangle and rectangle each have a perimeter of 14 centimeters. The hexagon has a perimeter of 12 centimeters.

23. Part A: 180: To find the total number of minutes he reads multiply 6 times 30 to get 180.
Part B: 3: An hour is 60 minutes, so if takes 180 and divide by 60 to get 3.

24. B: The total weight of the watermelons was 28, and if each one weighed the same then you can just divide by 7 to get 4 pounds each.

25. Part A: 32cm: The perimeter of a rectangle is the length of all of the sides added together. The length is 9 and the width is 7, but there are two lengths and two widths, so $7 + 7 + 9 + 9 = 32$ cm.

Part B: 63 cm: The area of a rectangle id length times width, so $7 \times 9 = 63$.

26. D: The thermometer shows 4 marks between each whole number, or 5 intervals. This means each interval on the thermometer represents 2 degrees since there are 5 intervals between each difference of 10 degrees. The thermometer reveals a reading at 4 degrees above 70 degrees (2 marks above 70), or 6 degrees below 80 degrees (3 marks below 80). Thus, the temperature outside is 74 degrees Fahrenheit.

27. B: There are 6 yellow cards and 3 red cards. The more cards there are of a certain color, the more likely it is that the color is drawn. With more yellow cards than red cards in the bag, he is more likely to draw a yellow card than a red card. There are more green cards than yellow cards, so he is more likely to draw a green card than a yellow card. There are less yellow cards than blue cards, so he is less likely to draw a yellow card than a blue card. Finally, the number of red, blue, green, and yellow cards are all different – so none of them are equally likely to be drawn compared to another color. Thus, Choice B is the only true statement.

28. D: Since the spinner only has sections, labeled 1 – 8, there is not a section, labeled "9". Therefore, it is impossible for the spinner to land on a 9.

29. C: Florida had 20 teachers that attended the event, which is less than the number of teachers who attended the event from each of the other three states. The number of teachers that attended the event from each of the other states were 40 (Arizona), 80 (New York), and 50 (California). Also, just looking at the bar graph shows that Florida had the least number of teachers attend compared to the other states because the bar is much lower in the graph.

30. The hamster received 10 votes and the fish received 2 votes. The difference is 10 – 2 = **8 votes**.

31. B: The number of blocks used in each tower increases by 2. Therefore, the number of blocks used in the next four towers can be found by adding

2 to the number of blocks in the 4th tower and continuing to add 2 blocks for each tower that comes next. This gives: 10, 12, 14, and 16, with 16 blocks used in the eighth tower.

32. D: The shapes all have at least 6 edges, with a triangular pyramid having 6 edges, a triangular prism having 9 edges, and a square pyramid having 8 edges. These shapes are clearly not all pyramids or all prisms, and they do not all have 5 faces (the triangular prism and square pyramid both have 5 faces but the triangular pyramid has only 4 faces). So, Choice D is the only statement common to all of the shapes.

33. B: The pencil is approximately 3.25 inches, which rounds to 3 inches.

34. A: The short hand, or hour hand, is between 10 o'clock and 11 o'clock, revealing that Amanda arrived after 10 o'clock, but before 11 o'clock. It is much closer to the 10, so this indicates the time is much closer to 10 o'clock than 11 o'clock. The long hand, or minute hand, is pointing to the 2, indicating 10 minutes after the hour. This is because for minutes, each number represents 5 minutes; so $2 \times 5 = 10$. So, she arrived at the party at 10:10.

35. D: The thermometer shows 4 marks between each whole number, or 5 intervals. This means each interval on the thermometer represents 2 degrees since there are 5 intervals between each difference of 10 degrees. The thermometer reveals a reading at 4 degrees above 70 degrees (2 marks above 70), or 6 degrees below 80 degrees (3 marks below 80). Thus, the temperature outside is 74 degrees Fahrenheit.

36. C: The more candy there is of a certain kind, the more likely it is that the candy is drawn. With more lollipops than chocolates in the bowl, she is more likely to draw a lollipop than a chocolate. There are more peppermints than chocolates, so she is more likely to draw a peppermint than a chocolate. There are more peppermints than lollipops, so she is more likely to draw a peppermint than a lollipop. Finally, the number of chocolates, peppermints, and lollipops are all different – so none of them are equally likely to be drawn compared to another color. Thus, Choice C is the only true statement.

37. A: Each car has 4 wheels, so the numbers of cars should be multiplied by 4 to find the total number of wheels. 3 cars will have 3 × 4 wheels, or 12 wheels, 4 cars will have 4 × 4 wheels, or 16 wheels, 7 cars will have 7 × 4 wheels, or 28 wheels, 11 cars will have 11 × 4 wheels, or 44 wheels, and 12 cars will have 12 × 4 wheels, or 48 wheels.

Science

Scientific method

The Steps of the Scientific Method
1. Find a topic to study or investigate. Usually this is in the form of a question. For example, do plants grow better with fertilizer?
2. Gather information about the topic. Read books or search for information on the Internet. Ask an expert in the field. Narrow the broad topic into a specific topic. For example, what is the effect of nitrogen fertilizer on the growth of bean plants?
3. Form a hypothesis or sensible guess that answers the question. Try to answer the question based on what was learned from the research. For example, I think that plants will grow the tallest using the amount of nitrogen fertilizer that is recommended by the manufacturer.
4. Design and perform an experiment to test the hypothesis. An experiment has an independent variable, dependent variable, several constants, and a control if possible. For example, the type of containers, soil, and plants as well as the amount of water and sunlight are the same for every trial of the experiment. Only the concentration of the fertilizer varies or changes.
5. Record the data during the experiment. Then study or analyze the data to determine the relationship between the independent variable and the dependent variable. This usually includes tables, charts, and graphs.
6. State the conclusion. Do the results support or contradict the original hypothesis?

Purpose and design of a good experiment

An experiment tests the hypothesis to discover if the hypothesis is true or false. An experiment includes an independent variable, a dependent variable, a control, and several constants. The independent variable is the factor that is changed or varied during the experiment. The dependent variable is the factor that is measured during the experiment. For example, for the hypothesis, ""If bean plants receive the recommended amount of nitrogen fertilizer, then the plants will grow the tallest," the independent variable is the concentration of nitrogen in the fertilizer. The dependent variable is the height of the plant. The control is part of the experiment in which there is no independent variable. The control is used for comparison. For example, the control is a group of plants that receives no fertilizer. The constants are factors that remain the same for all trials of the experiment, including the control. For example, constants include the amount of sunlight and the types of soil, container, and seeds.

Example
Describe an experiment to test the hypothesis, "If bean plants receive the recommended amount of nitrogen fertilizer, then the plants will grow the tallest."

Hypothesis - If bean plants receive the recommended amount of nitrogen fertilizer, then the plants will grow the tallest.

Experiment - The independent variable is the concentration of the fertilizer. The dependent variable is the height of the bean seedlings. The control is a group of seedlings that receive no fertilizer. The constants include the type of pot, soil, bean seedlings, temperature, humidity, and the amount of water and sunlight. Forty seedlings are divided into four groups of ten. Group 1 (the control group) receives no fertilizer. Group 2 receives half of the fertilizer recommended by the manufacturer. Group 3 receives the exact amount recommended by the manufacturer. Group 4 received twice the fertilizer recommended by the manufacturer. The heights of the plants are recorded every three days for six weeks.

ACT Aspire Reasoning Test

Tips for taking the ACT Aspire Reasoning Test

1. **Don't be scared by science terms or big words.** For many of the passages, you might not need to completely understand what is written in the paragraphs. Many of the questions are based only on your ability to read and take information from the graphs, charts, tables, figures, or illustrations. New words or difficult words are usually defined.
2. **The easiest questions usually come right after the passages.** After quickly reading the passage and skimming the charts or illustrations, see if you can answer the first question from each passage.
3. **Keep moving.** Don't spend more than one minute on any question. Keep moving. The easy questions are worth as many points as the harder questions. By spending too much time on the harder questions, you will miss the chance to gain points by answering the easy questions associated with passages you will never even read before the time is up.
4. **Work on the type of passages you think are the easiest first.** Be prepared. Know the types of passages and questions covered on this test. Read the passages you feel the most comfortable with first.
5. **Look for patterns or trends.** When you read through the passage and glance over the charts and figures, look for patterns or trends. As one variable increases, does the other variable increase or decrease? How does changing one factor affect another factor?

Topics and the types of passages covered on the ACT Aspire Science Reasoning Test

The ACT Aspire Science Reasoning Test covers a variety of science topics, including biology such as information about what affects the growth of plants, chemistry such as the pH scale, physics such as the effects of forces on motion, geology such as the different types of minerals, and astronomy such as information about the planets. Students are not expected to know specific or detailed knowledge of each topic. Instead, this test is designed to test your ability to read a scientific passage and find information from the charts, tables, graphs, and illustrations provided with the passage. Difficult terms are usually defined in the passage. Formulas are usually provided.

The ACT Aspire Science Reasoning Test includes three types of passages: data representation, research summaries, and conflicting viewpoints. In the data representation passages, a paragraph with charts, tables, figures, or illustrations is provided about a specific science topic. Students are expected to understand the passage and interpret the information in the charts, graphs, and other visual representations. In the research summary passages, details regarding an experiment and the data from that experiment are provided. Students need to understand, analyze, and interpret graphs and tables. Students need to understand the design of the experiment and interpret the results of the experiment. Students may be asked to make predictions. In the conflicting viewpoint passages, two or more opinions are presented about a scientific topic. Students need to recognize similarities and differences between the viewpoints.

ACT Aspire Science Reasoning Test

<u>Types of questions on the ACT Aspire Science Reasoning Test</u>
Each passage contains a paragraph and usually charts, tables, graphs, illustrations, or figures. This test is designed to test your ability to understand and use the information that is presented in the graphs and charts. To answer a question, you may simply need to read a term from a table or read data from a graph. The more difficult questions may ask for you to recognize patterns or trends. You may need to combine information from the graphs and charts in order to answer a question. Complex math calculations are not required. Usually you can use estimation to get a close answer and then select from the answers provided in the answer choices. You may have to draw inferences for graphs and figures or interpret coordinating tables.

Strategies for approaching the data representation passages

Tips for the Data Representation Passages

1. ***Don't be afraid of science passages.*** You don't have to completely understand the passages to answer the questions. Even if the terms and concepts seem hard, the questions are usually pretty easy.
2. ***Usually the easiest questions are first.*** After quickly reading the passage and skimming the charts or illustrations, see if you can answer the first question associated with each passage. Usually the easiest questions are first.
3. ***Keep moving!*** Don't spend more than one minute on any particular question. If you don't know the answer, guess and move on. By spending too much time on the harder questions, you will miss the opportunity to gain points by answering the easy questions associated with passages you will never reach before the time is up.
4. ***Problem-solving tips:*** Restate the problem in your own words. Ask yourself what information is needed. Find the information you need to answer the question.
5. ***Pattern, patterns, patterns.*** When you read through the passage and glance over the charts and figures, look for patterns or trends. Do two factors increase? Do two factors decrease? Does one factor increase while a different factor decreases?
6. ***Stick with the information in the passage.*** Don't use any outside science knowledge in answering the actual question. This science knowledge may help you understand the passage, but all the answers should be in the passage or inferred from the passage.

<u>Example</u>
Partial Passage: A magnet pulls on objects made of iron or other specific metals. The magnet has a magnetic field that is shown by the field lines in Figure 1. The actual field lines are invisible, but small pieces of iron called iron filings line up in paths resembling the field lines when sprinkled near the magnet. The magnetic field lines follow the path shown by the arrows. The south pole of the magnet is marked with the *S*. The north pole of the magnet is marked with the *N*.

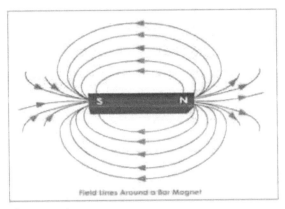
Field Lines Around a Bar Magnet

Figure 1

Question: Which of the following best describes the pattern of tiny iron filings sprinkled near a bar magnet?

    a. Loops drawn from the north pole to the south pole
    b. Straight lines drawn towards the magnet from every direction
    c. Circles drawn around the magnet but not touching the magnet
    d. Waves drawn back and forth between the north and south pole

Suggested Approach: According to Figure 1, the arrows on the field lines connected to the north pole are pointing away from the north pole. The arrows on the field lines connected to the south pole are pointing towards the south pole. Iron filings line up with the magnetic field line, which form loops from the north pole to the south pole. Therefore, choice A is correct.

<u>Example</u>

Partial Passage: The skin is the largest organ of the body. The skin is made up of three layers. The top layer is called the epidermis. The epidermis is made up of dead cells. The second layer of skin is called the dermis. The dermis is made up of live cells. Sweat glands and oil glands are located in the dermis. The third layer of the skin is called the subcutaneous layer. The subcutaneous layer helps to connect the skin to the muscle tissue underneath. See Figure 1.

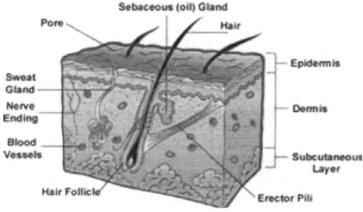

Figure 1

Question:

Which of the following lists the layers of the skin from outside of the skin to the inside of the skin?

    a. Dermis, subcutaneous layer, epidermis
    b. Epidermis, dermis, subcutaneous layer
    c. Subcutaneous layer, epidermis, dermis
    d. Epidermis, subcutaneous layer, dermis

Suggested Approach: The passage states the top layer of skin is the epidermis. The second layer of skin is the dermis. The third layer of skins is the subcutaneous layer. From Figure 1, the outside layer of the skin is the epidermis. The dermis lies beneath the epidermis. The subcutaneous layer lies beneath the dermis. Therefore, choice B is correct.

Research summary passages

<u>What to expect in the research summary passages</u>
In the research summary passages, details regarding an experiment and the data from that experiment are provided. Students need to understand, analyze, and interpret graphs and tables. Students need understand the design of the experiment and interpret the results of the experiment. Students may be asked to make predictions or inferences or to extrapolate. When reading about the experiment, ask these questions. What is being tested? Why is it being tested? What are the variables? What factors stay the same? Identify the independent variable and the dependent variable. Try to determine the relationship between these variables. Does one factor increase as another factor increases? Does one factor decrease as another factor decreases? Does one factor increase as another factor decreases? Be prepared to interpret data points and extrapolate data from tables and graphs. Remember, many of the questions can be answered by interpreting the charts and graphs without even reading the passage. When studying the graphs and charts, be sure to read all captions, keys, and labels. Identify the axes and the units.

<u>Example</u>
Partial Passage and Experiment. Students studied how altitude affects wind speed. Altitude is the distance from the surface of the Earth at sea level. Anemometers were placed at 1 meter, 2 meters, 3 meters, and 4 meters above the ground. Students counted the number of turns each anemometer turned in one minute. Students repeated the test the next two days. That data was also recorded in Table 1.

Table 1 Anemometer: Turns per Minute				
	Height from Ground			
Testing Day	**1 meter**	**2 meters**	**3 meters**	**4 meters**
Day 1	14	15	16	17
Day 2	16	17	18	19
Day 3	13	14	15	16

Question: From the data in Table 1, what is the effect of altitude on wind speed?

  a. As altitude increases, wind speed remains the same.
  b. As altitude increases, wind speed decreases.
  c. As altitude increases, wind speed increases.
  d. As altitude increases, wind speed increases and then decreases.

Suggested Approach: According to Table 1, as altitude increases, wind speed increases. This can be determined by scanning from left to right across any of the three days. The number of turns in each row increases as height from the ground increases. Therefore, choice C is correct.

Conflicting viewpoint passage

<u>What to expect in the conflicting viewpoint passage</u>
In the conflicting viewpoint passages, two or more viewpoints or opinions are presented regarding an observed phenomenon, scientific topic, or scientific concern. Students are expected to evaluate alternative theories, hypotheses, and viewpoints. Students need to compare the viewpoints and recognize and understand the similarities and differences between the viewpoints. Some questions will cover specific details about the viewpoint. Students might be asked to make inferences or draw reasonable conclusions from the information that is provided. Only one of these types of passages is on this test.

<u>Approach for the conflicting viewpoint passage</u>
  1. ***It doesn't matter who's right!*** When reading the opposing or conflicting viewpoints, stick to the facts in the passage. Don't worry about who you think is right or wrong.
  2. ***Ignore your own opinion!*** Your viewpoint doesn't matter. Just read the passage and get the information needed to answer the questions.
  3. ***Take shorthand notes.*** Jot down or underline the information that supports each viewpoint. Jot down or circle key points of each viewpoint. Only use information that is stated in the viewpoints.

4. ***Look for similarities and differences.*** Ask yourself how the conflicting viewpoints argue about the same concept or explain the same concept.

<u>Example</u>

Partial Passage: After going down the plastic slide at recess, Justin notices that his hair is standing on end. Justin asks his friends Olivia and Sophia why his hair is standing up.

Olivia's Viewpoint: Justin picked up electric charges when going down the slide. The electric charges traveled to the ends of his hair. Since like charges repel each other, the individual strands of his hair moved apart from each other, making his hair appear to stand on end.

Sophia's Viewpoint: Justin's hair did not pick up electric charges when going down the slide. His hair is standing on end due to some chemical his hair picked up while going down the slide. The chemical made his hair sticky, and that's why his hair is standing on end. Even if Justin's hair did pick up electric charges, like charges attract each other. Electric charges cannot possibly be the reason Justin's hair is standing on end.

Question: Another student claimed that Justin's hair picked up electrons while going down the slide. Since electrons all have negative charges, the electrons in Justin's hair repelled each other, causing Justin's hair to stand up. Which of the other students would agree this is a possibility?
   a. Olivia only
   b. Sophia only
   c. Both Olivia and Sophia
   d. Neither Olivia nor Sophia

Suggested Approach: Since negative charges are electric charges, Olivia would agree that Justin's hair may have picked up electrons. Since Sophia specifically stated that Justin's hair did not pick up electric charges, she would not agree that his hair picked up negative charges. Therefore, choice A is correct.

Example

Partial Passage: After going down the plastic slide at recess, Justin notices that his hair is standing on end. Justin asks why his hair is standing up. *Olivia's Viewpoint:* Justin picked up electric charges when going down the slide. Since like charges repel each other, the individual strands of his hair moved apart from each other. *Sophia's Viewpoint:* Justin's hair did not pick up electric charges when going down the slide. His hair is standing on end due to some chemical his hair picked up while going down the slide. The chemical made his hair sticky.

Question: One student claimed another student spilled a juice box on the slide. Based on the passage, does this support Sophia's viewpoint?

a. Yes; Sophia stated that Justin's hair picked up juice as he went down the slide.

b. Yes; Sophia stated that Justin's hair picked up a chemical. This chemical could have been juice from the juice box.

c. No; Sophia stated that Justin's hair picked up electric charges, not chemicals.

d. No; Sophia stated Justin's hair did not pick up any chemicals.

Suggested Approach: Sophia said that Justin's hair picked up chemicals that made his hair sticky. Since juice can be sticky, this claim supports Sophia's viewpoint. Therefore, choice B is correct

Practice Test

Practice Questions

Use the following information for Questions 1-6.

Most plants begin life as a tiny seed. When the conditions are favorable, the seed sprouts. A tiny root and shoot emerge from the seed in a process called germination. The young plant now called a seedling continues to grow and mature. When the plant is able to reproduce, the seedling becomes an adult. The adult plant reproduces, and new seeds are formed. The life cycle begins again (see Figure 1).

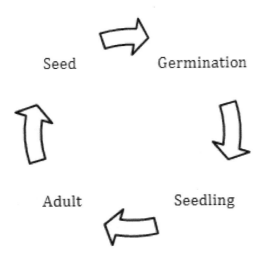

Seed   Germination

Adult   Seedling

Figure 1: Life Cycle of a Plant

Students studied the effect of temperature on the germination of seeds from one type of plant.

Study

Students placed potting soil in 30 paper cups, and then planted a seed in each cup. The 30 cups were divided into three groups of 10 cups each. One group was kept at 15°C. Another group was kept at 20°C. The last group was kept at 25°C. The students monitored the moisture of the soil, and added water as needed to maintain moist soil. First, they recorded the number of days until each plant sprouted out of the top of the soil. Then they recorded the height of the plants in centimeters once a week for the next two weeks. The students presented the average number of days to sprout and the average heights of the seedlings of each group at one week and two weeks in the table.

Temperature (°C)	Average number of days to sprout	Average height at 1 week after sprouting (cm)	Average height at 2 weeks after sprouting (cm)
15	16	1.0	2.0
20	11	1.5	3.0
25	8	2.0	4.0

1. According to the table, what was the average number of days to sprout for the seeds kept at 25°C?

Ⓐ 16

Ⓑ 11

Ⓒ 8

Ⓓ 2.0

2. According to the table, what was the average height in centimeters of the seedlings kept at 15°C at 2 weeks after sprouting?

Ⓐ 4.0

Ⓑ 3.0

Ⓒ 1.0

Ⓓ 2.0

3. Using the results in the table, as the temperature increased, the average number of days to sprout _____.

   Ⓐ decreased

   Ⓑ increased

   Ⓒ stayed the same

   Ⓓ increased, then decreased

4. Using the results in the table, at the end of 2 weeks, which group of plants was the tallest?

   Ⓐ The ones kept at 10 °C

   Ⓑ The ones kept at 15 °C

   Ⓒ The ones kept at 20 °C

   Ⓓ The ones kept at 25 °C

5. During the study, what was the factor that varied or changed?

   Ⓐ Soil

   Ⓑ Temperature

   Ⓒ Container

   Ⓓ Seed

6. Based on the information from this study, if the students were to do another study with the same type of seeds, soil, and containers, but add a fourth group kept at 10°C, which of the following would most likely be true?

Ⓐ The seeds kept at 10°C would take the same amount of time to sprout as the seeds kept at 20°C.

Ⓑ The seeds kept at 10°C would take longer to sprout than the seeds kept at 15°C.

Ⓒ The seeds kept at 10°C would take less time to sprout than the seeds kept at 25°C.

Ⓓ The seeds kept at 10°C would take less time to sprout than the seeds kept at 20°C.

Use the following information for Questions 7-12.

Matter exists in three common forms: solids, liquids, and gases. In solids, the particles of the substance are close together and held in place. Solids have a specific shape and volume. In liquids, the particles are farther apart and slide over each other. Liquids flow and take the shape of their containers. In gases, the particles are very far apart and free to move away from one another. Gases have no specific shape and fill their containers. See Figure 1. Matter can change from one form to another. If a solid substance is heated, it can change into a liquid. If a liquid substance is heated, it can change into a gas. If a gas is cooled, it can change into a liquid. If a liquid is cooled, it can change into a solid. Each of these changes has a special name. For example, when a solid is changed into a liquid, the process is called melting. Scientists may refer to heat as energy or enthalpy. See Figure 2.

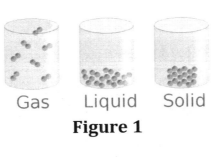

Gas   Liquid   Solid

Figure 1

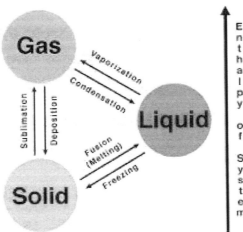

Figure 2

7. In which common state of matter are the particles the farthest apart?

Ⓐ Solid

Ⓑ Liquid

Ⓒ Gas

Ⓓ Plasma

8. Which of the following correctly describes a solid substance?

Ⓐ The particles of a solid remain in their positions.

Ⓑ The particles of a solid move farther and farther apart.

Ⓒ The particles of a solid are free to flow.

Ⓓ The particles of solid slide over each other.

9. Which of the following describes the effect of adding heat to an ice cube?

Ⓐ The ice cube melts to form water.

Ⓑ The ice cube freezes to form water.

Ⓒ The ice cube boils to form water.

Ⓓ The ice cube condenses to form water.

10. Which of the following can be described as a substance changing from the gaseous state to the liquid state?

Ⓐ The particles of the substance move faster.

Ⓑ The particles of the substance float away.

Ⓒ The particles of the substance become fixed in place.

Ⓓ The particles of the substance move closer together.

11. Which of the following correctly describes the process of sublimation?

Ⓐ When a liquid changes into a solid

Ⓑ When a solid changes into a gas

Ⓒ When a liquid changes into a gas

Ⓓ When a gas changes into a liquid

12. A student forgets a chocolate bar on the school bus seat on a hot day in May. When she returns to the bus at the end of the day, which if the following describes what most likely happened to her chocolate bar?

Ⓐ The chocolate bar melted.

Ⓑ The chocolate bar froze.

Ⓒ The chocolate bar disappeared.

Ⓓ The chocolate bar changed to the gaseous state.

Use the following information for Questions 13-18.

Energy can be transferred from one object to another. This transfer of energy is known as heat. Heat transfer occurs by conduction, convection, and radiation. See Figure 1. In conduction, the two objects actually touch. Heat is transferred from hot pavement to a bare foot through conduction. The energy is transferred from molecule to molecule as they vibrate against each other. In convection, the energy is transferred by moving currents. When liquids or gases are heated, the warmed area rises. Cooler areas of these liquids and gases sink. Heat is transferred by the moving liquids or gases. Heat travels through water by convection currents. In radiation, heat is transferred by energy waves. These energy waves can travel through space or can travel right through matter. Energy reaches us from the sun by radiation.

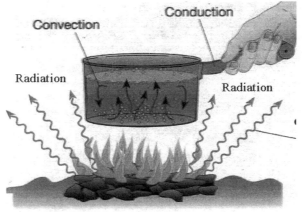

Figure 1

Students studied the effect of convection on the temperature at various locations in the classroom.

Study

Students placed thermometers at heights of 1 meter, 2 meters, and 3 meters in the science room. The students recorded the temperature in degrees Celsius at the beginning of class for 10 days. The students graphed the average temperatures at each height in Figure 2.

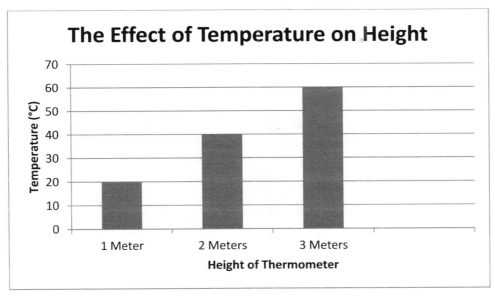

Figure 2

13. Which of the following describes the conduction as shown in Figure 1?

Ⓐ Heat is transferred from the fire to the person's hand by direct contact.

Ⓑ Heat is transferred from the fire to the pan by direct contact.

Ⓒ Heat is transferred throughout the water by direct contact.

Ⓓ Heat is transferred from the handle to the person's hand by direct contact.

14. A student accidently touches a light bulb, and pulls his hand away quickly to avoid a severe burn. Which of the following terms describes the heat transfer to the student's hand?

Ⓐ Radiation

Ⓑ Convection

Ⓒ Conduction

Ⓓ Condensation

15. Students decide to use a heating lamp to keep baby chicks warm by placing the heating lamp at the correct height above the pen for the baby chicks. Which of the following describes how a heating lamp warms baby chicks?

Ⓐ The heat will not reach the baby chicks.

Ⓑ The heat is transferred to the baby chicks by radiation.

Ⓒ The heat is transferred to the baby chicks by conduction.

Ⓓ The heat is transferred to the baby chicks by convection.

16. Which of the following describes the trend in Figure 2?

Ⓐ As the height of the thermometer increases, the temperature drops to zero.

Ⓑ As the height of the thermometer increases, the temperature stays the same.

Ⓒ As the height of the thermometer increases, the temperature decreases.

Ⓓ As the height of the thermometer increases, the temperature increases.

17. Which of the following most likely explains the reason for the temperature nearest the ceiling?

Ⓐ Conduction cooled the air near the ceiling.

Ⓑ Conduction warmed the air near the ceiling.

Ⓒ Convection currents carried warm air up to the ceiling.

Ⓓ Convection currents cooled the air near the ceiling.

18. What is the average temperature recorded at a height of 2 meters?

Ⓐ 40°C

Ⓑ 20°C

Ⓒ 80°C

Ⓓ 60°C

Use the following information for Questions 19-24.

The Earth, moon, and sun system describes the motion of the Earth as it travels or revolves around the sun and the motion of the moon as it travels or revolves around the Earth. The Earth revolves around the sun once every 365 ¼ days, which is called a year. The moon revolves around the Earth once nearly every 27 days, which is called a month. See Figure 1. The Earth is tilted on its axis at 23.5°. This tilt of the Earth's axis causes many areas to experience the four seasons called spring, summer, fall, and winter. The Earth rotates about its axis about once every 24 hours, which is called a day. This rotation of the Earth causes an area to have day and night. When an area is facing towards the sun, it is daytime. When an area is facing away from the sun, it is nighttime. See Figure 2.

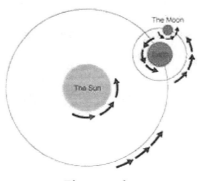

Figure 1

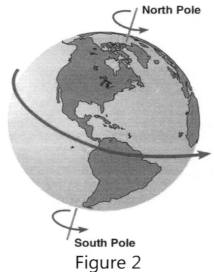

North Pole

South Pole

Figure 2

19. What causes day and night?

Ⓐ The Earth's rotation

Ⓑ The tilt of the Earth's axis

Ⓒ The moon blocking the sun

Ⓓ The tilt of the sun

20. Which of the following best describes the axis of the Earth?

Ⓐ The imaginary line around the middle of the Earth

Ⓑ The imaginary line that the Earth spins upon

Ⓒ The imaginary line through the middle of the moon

Ⓓ The imaginary line that the sun spins upon

21. Why do seasons change?

Ⓐ Because the sun is far from the Earth

Ⓑ Because the sun is spinning

Ⓒ Because the Earth is tilted

Ⓓ Because the moon is nearby

22. What is the length of time it takes the Earth to spin once upon its axis called?

Ⓐ One year

Ⓑ One month

Ⓒ One day

Ⓓ One week

23. Which of the following lists the terms from shortest length of time to the longest length of time?

Ⓐ Day, month, week, year

Ⓑ Year, month, week, day

Ⓒ Week, day, month, year

Ⓓ Day, week, month, year

24. A student observes a top spinning on a table top. The student compares the motion of the top to the motion of the Earth. Which of the following terms describe the spinning motion of the top?

Ⓐ Revolving

Ⓑ Rotating

Ⓒ Shaking

Ⓓ Wobbling

Use the following information for Questions 25-30.

The skin is the largest organ of the body. The skin that covers and protects the body helps our bodies stay the right temperature. Also, the skin allows us to feel the sense of touch. The skin is made up of three layers. The top layer is called the epidermis. This is the part of the skin we can see. The epidermis is made up of dead cells. The second layer of skin is called the dermis. The dermis is just beneath the epidermis. The dermis is made up of live cells. Sweat glands and oil glands, as well as touch, pain, and temperature sensors, are located in the dermis. The third layer of the skin is called the subcutaneous layer. The subcutaneous layer is just beneath the dermis. The subcutaneous layer contains the base of the hair follicles and a layer of fat. This fat helps us stay warm. The subcutaneous layer helps to connect the skin to the muscle tissue underneath. See Figure 1.

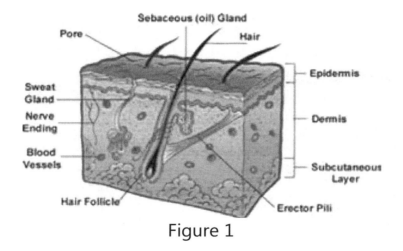

Figure 1

25. Which of the following lists the layers of the skin from outside of the skin to the inside of the skin?

Ⓐ Dermis, subcutaneous layer, epidermis

Ⓑ Epidermis, dermis, subcutaneous layer

Ⓒ Subcutaneous layer, epidermis, dermis

Ⓓ Epidermis, subcutaneous layer, dermis

26. According to the diagram, the pores of the sweat glands are located in which layer of the skin?

Ⓐ Subcutaneous layer

Ⓑ Dermis

Ⓒ Epidermis

Ⓓ Fatty layer

27. According to this diagram, which gland is attached to the hair follicle?

Ⓐ Sweat gland

Ⓑ Nerve ending

Ⓒ Blood vessel

Ⓓ Sebaceous gland

28. Which of the following is the best description of the skin?

Ⓐ The skin is made of soft, flexible layers of tissue.

Ⓑ The skin is made of one layer of tough tissue.

Ⓒ The skin is made of hard layers of bone tissue.

Ⓓ The skin is made of one thick layer of fat.

29. A student touches a warm mug of hot chocolate. How does the student sense that the mug is warm?

Ⓐ Sebaceous glands in the skin send a message to the brain.

Ⓑ Sweat glands in the skin send a message to the epidermis.

Ⓒ Temperature sensors in the skin send a message to the brain.

Ⓓ Hair follicles in the skin send a message to the subcutaneous layer.

30. Which of the following words best describes the type of cells located at the surface of the skin?

Ⓐ Live

Ⓑ Fat

Ⓒ Dead

Ⓓ Nerve

Use the following information for Questions 31-36.

A push or a pull is called a force. Forces can start or stop motion. Unbalanced forces result in motion. Balanced forces do not result in motion. Forces can speed up motion or slow down motion. The greater the force applied to an object, the greater the speed of the object.

Friction is a force that is opposite to motion. Friction slows an object down. Friction is caused by objects rubbing against each other.

Students studied how the type of surface affects the speed of a toy car as it rolls down a ramp.

Study

Students obtained four ramps of equal length with different surfaces: carpet, sandpaper, metal, and wood. Students raised the ends of the ramps to equal heights and placed identical toys cars at the top of each ramp. Students released the cars and used stopwatches to measure the amount of time it took each car to reach the end of the ramp. The students completed three trials and recorded their data in the table below.

Ramp Material	Time in seconds		
	Trial 1	Trial 2	Trial 3
Carpet	4.3	4.4	4.2
Sandpaper	6.2	6.3	6.2
Metal	2.5	2.6	2.4
Wood	3.7	3.7	3.6

31. Which of the following statements is NOT true?

Ⓐ Forces can start motion.

Ⓑ Forces can stop motion.

Ⓒ Forces can speed an object up.

Ⓓ Friction can speed an object up.

32. If a sled is sliding to the right, which of the following describes the direction of the friction on the sled?

Ⓐ To the left

Ⓑ To the right

Ⓒ Up

Ⓓ Down

33. Why was it important that the students use identical cars for all of the trials?

Ⓐ To make sure only the ramp material is changed

Ⓑ To make sure the wheels were made of different material

Ⓒ To make sure the cars roll at different speeds

Ⓓ To make sure that the stop watches were used correctly

34. Which of the following is NOT a force?

Ⓐ The distance a car moves

Ⓑ A tug on a rope

Ⓒ A shove on a box

Ⓓ Friction on a truck tire

35. Which of the following relates the time for the car to travel down the ramp to the type of material on the ramp?

Ⓐ The ramp with the fastest travel times had the material that had the most friction.

Ⓑ The ramp with the slowest travel times had the material that had the most friction.

Ⓒ The ramp with the fastest travel times was raised the highest.

Ⓓ The type of material had no effect on the travel times down the ramp.

36. Which of the ramp materials provided the least amount of friction?

Ⓐ Wood

Ⓑ Carpet

Ⓒ Sandpaper

Ⓓ Metal

Answers and Explanations

1. C: From the second column and third row of the table, the average number of days to sprout at 25 °C was 8 days. Therefore, choice C is correct.

2. D: From the fourth column and first row of the table, the average height of the seedlings kept at 15 °C at 2 weeks after sprouting was 2.0 cm. Therefore, choice D is correct.

3. A: From the second column of the table, the number of days to sprout decreased from 16 to 11 to 8 as the temperature increased. Therefore, choice A is correct.

4. D: From the fourth column of the table, the average height of the plants at the end of 2 weeks for 15°C, 20°C, and 25°C were 2.0 cm, 3.0 cm, and 4.0 cm, respectively. The plants kept at 25°C were the tallest. Therefore, choice D is correct.

5. B: It was stated that the students used the same type of soil, seeds, and containers. They studied the effect of temperature on germination. Therefore, choice B is correct.

6. B: Based on the information in the table, the lower the temperature, the longer it takes the seeds to sprout. If the seeds are kept at 10°C, it should take them longer to sprout than any of the seeds kept at the other temperatures. Therefore, choice B is correct.

7. C: In solids, the particles are close together. In liquids, since the particles have more energy, the particles are farther apart. In gases, since the particles have even more energy, the particles are the farthest apart. Therefore, choice C is correct.

8. A: The particles in a solid have less energy than those in liquids and gases. While these particles shake or vibrate, they remain in their positions.

The particles of a solid are not free to slide, flow, or move farther and farther apart. Therefore, choice A is correct.

9. A: Adding heat is the same as increasing energy, or enthalpy. If energy is added to an ice cube, the particles will gain energy and move farther apart to form a liquid. This process is called melting. Therefore, choice A is correct.

10. D: When a substance changes from a liquid to a gaseous state, the particles have less energy. Since the particles have less energy, they move closer together. Therefore, choice D is correct.

11. B: In Figure 2, the arrow that is drawn from the solid state to the gaseous state is labelled *sublimation.* Therefore, choice B is correct.

12. A: A chocolate bar is a solid. On a hot day, the temperature in the bus increased. As the temperature increases, a solid increases in energy and may change to a liquid state. In this situation, the chocolate bar melted. Therefore, choice A is correct.

13. D: Since the person's hand is in direct contact with the panhandle, heat is transferred from the handle to the person's hand by conduction. Therefore, choice D is correct.

14. C: When the student touches the light bulb, heat is transferred to the student's hand by direct contact through conduction. Therefore, choice C is correct.

15. B: Since the heating lamp is located above the baby chicks, the heat cannot be transferred to the chicks by convection. Instead, the heat travels to the chicks in energy waves by radiation. Therefore, choice B is correct.

16. D: In Figure 2, as the height increases from 1 meter to 2 meters to 3 meters, the bars representing the temperature get taller and taller. This means that the temperature is increasing. Therefore, choice D is correct.

17. C: The air in the room is a gas. Heat can be transferred in gases by moving air called convection currents. These convection currents carried warm air up to the ceiling. Therefore, choice C is correct.

18. A: The bar for 2 meters is in the middle of the graph. Reading the value from the left axis, the average temperature is 40°C. Therefore, choice A is correct.

19. A: The Earth's rotation causes day and night. When an area faces the sun, it is daytime. When an area faces away from the sun, it is nighttime. Therefore, choice A is correct.

20. B: The Earth spins upon an imaginary line that runs through it called an axis. Therefore, choice B is correct.

21. C: Because the Earth is tilted, different regions away from the equator experience different seasons as the Earth revolves around the sun. Therefore, choice C is correct.

22. C: The Earth spins upon its axis once every 24 hours, which is called a day. Therefore, Choice C is correct.

23. D: One day is a 24-hour period. One week is equal to 7 days. One month is about 27 days. One year is a little over 365 days. From shortest to longest these are day, week, month, and year. Therefore, choice D is correct.

24. B: The Earth rotates as it turns or spins about its axis. The top is spinning or rotating. Therefore, choice B is correct.

25. B: The outside layer of the skin is the epidermis. The dermis lies beneath the epidermis. The subcutaneous layer lies beneath the dermis. Therefore, choice B is correct.

26. C: From the diagram, the pores are drawn on the top layer of the skin. The top layer of the skin is the epidermis. Therefore, choice C is correct.

27. D: The diagram shows that the hair, erector pili, and sebaceous gland are attached to the hair follicle. Therefore, choice D is correct.

28. A: The skin is made up of three layers of soft tissue. The layers are soft and flexible. Therefore, choice A is correct.

29. C: The sense of touch is due to the temperature sensors in the dermis layer. The temperature sensors detect the warmth of the mug and send a message through a nerve to the brain. Therefore, the correct choice is C.

30. C: The surface of the skin is the epidermis. The cells that make up the epidermis are dead. Therefore, choice C is correct.

31. D: Friction is a force that acts opposite to the direction of motion. Friction slows an object down. Therefore, the correct choice is D.

32. A: Friction is a force that acts opposite to the direction of motion. If a sled is moving to the right, friction will act to the left. Therefore, the correct choice is A.

33. A: A good experiment or study can only have one variable. The variable in this study was the type of material on the ramp. The students used identical cars to make sure that only the type of material on the ramp varied. Therefore, choice A is correct.

34. A: A force is a push or a pull. Friction is a force that is opposite to the direction of motion. A tug is a pull. A shove is a push. Distance is not a push or a pull. Therefore, the correct choice is A.

35. B: The ramp with the fastest travel time had the metal surface. The ramp with the slowest travel time had the sandpaper surface. Sandpaper had much more friction than the metal. Therefore, choice B is correct.

36. D: Since the travel time for the metal was the fastest, the metal provided less friction than the other materials. Therefore, choice D is correct.

Success Strategies

The most important thing you can do is to ignore your fears and jump into the test immediately- do not be overwhelmed by any strange-sounding terms. You have to jump into the test like jumping into a pool- all at once is the easiest way.

Make Predictions

As you read and understand the question, try to guess what the answer will be. Remember that several of the answer choices are wrong, and once you begin reading them, your mind will immediately become cluttered with answer choices designed to throw you off. Your mind is typically the most focused immediately after you have read the question and digested its contents. If you can, try to predict what the correct answer will be. You may be surprised at what you can predict.

Quickly scan the choices and see if your prediction is in the listed answer choices. If it is, then you can be quite confident that you have the right answer. It still won't hurt to check the other answer choices, but most of the time, you've got it!

Answer the Question

It may seem obvious to only pick answer choices that answer the question, but the test writers can create some excellent answer choices that are wrong. Don't pick an answer just because it sounds right, or you believe it to be true. It MUST answer the question. Once you've made your selection, always go back and check it against the question and make sure that you didn't misread the question, and the answer choice does answer the question posed.

Benchmark

After you read the first answer choice, decide if you think it sounds correct or not. If it doesn't, move on to the next answer choice. If it does, mentally mark that answer choice. This doesn't mean that you've definitely selected it as your answer choice, it just means that it's the best you've seen thus far. Go ahead and read the next choice. If the next choice is worse than the one you've already selected, keep going to the next answer choice. If the next choice is better than the choice you've already selected, mentally mark the new answer choice as your best guess.

The first answer choice that you select becomes your standard. Every other answer choice must be benchmarked against that standard. That choice is correct until proven otherwise by another answer choice beating it out. Once you've decided that no other answer choice seems as good, do one final check to ensure that your answer choice answers the question posed.

Valid Information

Don't discount any of the information provided in the question. Every piece of information may be necessary to determine the correct answer. None of the information in the question is there to throw you off (while the answer choices will certainly have information to throw you off). If two seemingly unrelated topics are discussed, don't ignore either. You can be confident there is a relationship, or it wouldn't be included in the question, and you are probably going to have to determine what is that relationship to find the answer.

Avoid "Fact Traps"

Don't get distracted by a choice that is factually true. Your search is for the answer that answers the question. Stay focused and don't fall for an answer that is true but incorrect. Always go back to the question and make sure you're choosing an answer that actually answers the question and is not just a true statement. An answer can be factually correct, but it MUST answer the question asked. Additionally, two answers can both be seemingly correct, so be sure to read all of the answer choices, and make sure that you get the one that BEST answers the question.

Milk the Question

Some of the questions may throw you completely off. They might deal with a subject you have not been exposed to, or one that you haven't reviewed in years. While your lack of knowledge about the subject will be a hindrance, the question itself can give you many clues that will help you find the correct answer. Read the question carefully and look for clues. Watch particularly for adjectives and nouns describing difficult terms or words that you don't recognize. Regardless of if you completely understand a word or not, replacing it with a synonym either provided or one you more familiar with may help you to understand what the questions are asking. Rather than wracking your mind about specific detailed information concerning a difficult term or word, try to use mental substitutes that are easier to understand.

The Trap of Familiarity

Don't just choose a word because you recognize it. On difficult questions, you may not recognize a number of words in the answer choices. The test writers don't put "make-believe" words on the test; so don't think that just because you only recognize all the words in one answer choice means that answer choice must be correct. If you only recognize words in one answer choice, then focus on that one. Is it correct? Try your best to determine if it is correct. If it is, that is great, but if it doesn't, eliminate it. Each word and answer choice you eliminate increases your chances of getting the question correct, even if you then have to guess among the unfamiliar choices.

Eliminate Answers

Eliminate choices as soon as you realize they are wrong. But be careful! Make sure you consider all of the possible answer choices. Just because one appears right, doesn't mean that the next one won't be even better! The test writers will usually put more than one good answer choice for every question, so read all of them. Don't worry if you are stuck between two that seem right. By getting down to just two remaining possible choices, your odds are now 50/50. Rather than wasting too much time, play the odds. You are guessing, but guessing wisely, because you've been able to knock out some of the answer choices that you know are wrong. If you are eliminating choices and realize that the last answer choice you are left with is also obviously wrong, don't panic. Start over and consider each choice again. There may easily be something that you missed the first time and will realize on the second pass.

Tough Questions

If you are stumped on a problem or it appears too hard or too difficult, don't waste time. Move on! Remember though, if you can quickly check for obviously incorrect answer choices, your chances of guessing correctly are greatly improved. Before you completely give up, at least try to knock out a couple of possible answers. Eliminate what you can and then guess at the remaining answer choices before moving on.

Brainstorm

If you get stuck on a difficult question, spend a few seconds quickly brainstorming. Run through the complete list of possible answer choices. Look at each choice and ask yourself, "Could this answer the question satisfactorily?" Go through each answer choice and consider it independently of the other. By systematically going through all possibilities, you may find something that you would otherwise overlook. Remember that when you get stuck, it's important to try to keep moving.

Read Carefully

Understand the problem. Read the question and answer choices carefully. Don't miss the question because you misread the terms. You have plenty of time to read each question thoroughly and make sure you understand what is being asked. Yet a happy medium must be attained, so don't waste too much time. You must read carefully, but efficiently.

Face Value

When in doubt, use common sense. Always accept the situation in the problem at face value. Don't read too much into it. These problems will not require you to make huge leaps of logic. The test writers aren't trying to throw you off with a cheap trick. If you have to go beyond creativity and make a leap of logic in order to have an answer choice answer the question, then you should look at the other answer choices. Don't overcomplicate the problem by creating theoretical relationships or explanations that will warp time or space. These are normal problems rooted in reality. It's just that the applicable relationship or explanation may not be readily apparent and you have to figure things out. Use your common sense to interpret anything that isn't clear.

Prefixes

If you're having trouble with a word in the question or answer choices, try dissecting it. Take advantage of every clue that the word might include. Prefixes and suffixes can be a huge help. Usually they allow you to determine a basic meaning. Pre- means before, post- means after, pro - is positive, de- is negative. From these prefixes and suffixes, you can get an idea of the general meaning of the word and try to put it into context. Beware though of any traps. Just because con is the opposite of pro, doesn't necessarily mean congress is the opposite of progress!

Hedge Phrases

Watch out for critical "hedge" phrases, such as likely, may, can, will often, sometimes, often, almost, mostly, usually, generally, rarely, sometimes. Question writers insert these hedge phrases to cover every possibility. Often an answer choice will be wrong simply because it leaves no room for exception. Avoid answer choices that have definitive words like "exactly," and "always".

Switchback Words

Stay alert for "switchbacks". These are the words and phrases frequently used to alert you to shifts in thought. The most common switchback word is "but". Others include although, however, nevertheless, on the other hand, even though, while, in spite of, despite, regardless of.

New Information

Correct answer choices will rarely have completely new information included. Answer choices typically are straightforward reflections of the material asked about and will directly relate to the question. If a new piece of information is included in an answer choice that doesn't even seem to relate to the topic being asked about, then that answer choice is likely incorrect.   All of the information needed to answer the question is usually provided for you, and so you should not have to make guesses that are unsupported or choose answer choices that require unknown information that cannot be reasoned on its own.

Time Management

On technical questions, don't get lost on the technical terms. Don't spend too much time on any one question. If you don't know what a term means, then since you don't have a dictionary, odds are you aren't going to get much further. You should immediately recognize terms as whether or not you know them. If you don't, work with the other clues that you have, the other answer choices and terms provided, but don't waste too much time trying to figure out a difficult term.

Contextual Clues

Look for contextual clues. An answer can be right but not correct. The contextual clues will help you find the answer that is most right and is correct. Understand the context in which a phrase or statement is made. This will help you make important distinctions.

Don't Panic

Panicking will not answer any questions for you. Therefore, it isn't helpful. When you first see the question, if your mind goes blank, take a deep breath.   Force yourself to mechanically go through the steps of solving the problem and using the strategies you've learned.

Pace Yourself

Don't get clock fever. It's easy to be overwhelmed when you're looking at a page full of questions, your mind is full of random thoughts and feeling confused, and the clock is ticking down faster than you would like. Calm down and maintain the pace that you have set for yourself. As long as you are on track by monitoring your pace, you are guaranteed to have enough time for yourself. When you get to the last few minutes of the test, it may seem like you won't have enough time left, but if you only have as many questions as you should have left at that point, then you're right on track!

Answer Selection

The best way to pick an answer choice is to eliminate all of those that are wrong, until only one is left and confirm that is the correct answer. Sometimes though, an answer choice may immediately look right. Be careful! Take a second to make sure that the other choices are not equally obvious. Don't make a hasty mistake. There are only two times that you should stop before checking other answers. First is when you are positive that the answer choice you have selected is correct. Second is when time is almost out and you have to make a quick guess!

Check Your Work

Since you will probably not know every term listed and the answer to every question, it is important that you get credit for the ones that you do know. Don't miss any questions through careless mistakes. If at all possible, try to take a second to look back over your answer selection and make sure you've selected the correct answer choice and haven't made a costly careless mistake (such as marking an answer choice that you didn't mean to mark). This quick double check should more than pay for itself in caught mistakes for the time it costs.

Beware of Directly Quoted Answers

Sometimes an answer choice will repeat word for word a portion of the question or reference section. However, beware of such exact duplication – it may be a trap! More than likely, the correct choice will paraphrase or summarize a point, rather than being exactly the same wording.

Slang

Scientific sounding answers are better than slang ones. An answer choice that begins "To compare the outcomes..." is much more likely to be correct than one that begins "Because some people insisted..."

Extreme Statements

Avoid wild answers that throw out highly controversial ideas that are proclaimed as established fact. An answer choice that states the "process should be used in certain situations, if..." is much more likely to be correct than one that states the "process should be discontinued completely." The first is a calm rational statement and doesn't even make a definitive, uncompromising stance, using a hedge word "if" to provide wiggle room, whereas the second choice is a radical idea and far more extreme.

Answer Choice Families

When you have two or more answer choices that are direct opposites or parallels, one of them is usually the correct answer. For instance, if one answer choice states "x increases" and another answer choice states "x decreases" or "y increases," then those two or three answer choices are very similar in construction and fall into the same family of answer choices. A family of answer choices is when two or three answer choices are very similar in construction, and yet often have a directly opposite meaning. Usually the correct answer choice will be in that family of answer choices. The "odd man out" or answer choice that doesn't seem to fit the parallel construction of the other answer choices is more likely to be incorrect.

Workbook Answer Keys and Additional Bonus Material

Due to our efforts to try to keep this book to a manageable length, we've created a link that will give you access to all of your additional bonus material.

Please visit http://www.mometrix.com/bonus948/actaspireg3 to access the information.